A CHRISTIAN'S
RESPONSE TO ISLAM

By
William McElwee Miller

Presbyterian and Reformed Publishing Company
Phillipsburg, New Jersey 08865

DEDICATION

To my beloved wife
Isabelle
who for more than fifty years
has shared my joys and sorrows

CONTENTS

1

That They May Be Saved

THAT THEY MAY BE SAVED

"My heart's desire and prayer to God for them is that they may be saved!" So spoke one who had a passion for souls, and who longed for the salvation of those very dear to him. Who was this lover of the lost? A father who yearned that his beloved children might have life in Christ? A devoted pastor who longed and labored that not one of his flock should perish? No, he whose heart's desire was the salvation of others was the greatest missionary who ever lived, the Apostle Paul. And those for whose salvation he prayed were not his friends but his enemies, his own people the Jews who had everywhere rejected him.

Paul had travelled far to find the Jews and tell them the Good News of the coming of the Messiah to save them, but in Damascus and Antioch and Iconium, in Thessalonica and Corinth and Ephesus, most of the Israelites who heard his message refused to believe. In five of their synagogues they had inflicted on his bare back the thirty-nine legal lashes, and they had frequently sought to kill him. But instead of asking God to destroy them he had sought their salvation. Not only was it his heartfelt desire that they be saved, he was even willing to be damned himself if that would cause them to be forgiven and accepted by God. In his Epistle to the Romans he wrote thus about the people who hated him so bitterly: "My heart's desire and prayer to God for them is that they may be saved. . . . I am speaking the truth in Christ, I am not lying, I have great sorrow and unceasing anguish in my heart. For I could wish that I myself were accursed and cut off from Christ for the sake of my brethren, my kindred by race" (Rom. 10:1; 9:1-3). And so, constrained by the love of Christ, Paul continued to agonize in prayer for his people who had refused to believe the Good News of salvation.

Paul's willingness to be cut off from Christ if that would cause the Jews to be grafted into Christ reminds us of the prayer of Moses the man of God when the people of Israel made the golden calf and worshiped it. He cried out to God: "Alas, this people have sinned a great sin, they have made for themselves gods of gold. But now, if thou wilt forgive their sin—and if not, blot me, I pray thee, out of thy book which thou hast written" (Ex. 32:31-32). Moses felt he could not live if his people perished. God heard his plea and forgave his people, and brought them at last into the Promised Land.

We are reminded also of a prayer offered several hundred years before the time of Moses by Abraham, the great father of the faithful and the friend of God. The prayer was not for Isaac, the son of Sarah his wife whom God had promised to him, but for Ishmael, the son of Hagar the Egyptian slave-girl, whom she had borne to Abra-

4

ham. Great were the blessings which God promised to Isaac and to his descendants, through whom the knowledge of God and the gift of salvation were to come to the world. Abraham believed God and rejoiced in God's covenant and his gracious promises regarding Isaac.

But Abraham loved his older son Ishmael (meaning "God hears"), whom God had given to him in answer to his request for a son. And so Abraham prayed for Ishmael, and said to God, "Oh that Ishmael might live in thy sight!" God heard this request, and said to Abraham: "As for Ishmael, I have heard you; behold, I will bless him and make him fruitful and multiply him exceedingly; he shall be the father of twelve princes, and I will make him a great nation. But I will establish my covenant with Isaac" (Gen. 17: 18-21). Thus God gave his blessing to both of Abraham's sons and their descendants.

We know who the descendants of Isaac are; they are Jacob and his twelve sons and the "children of Israel" who were born to them. One of them was Jesus Christ, the Saviour of the world. But who are the descendants of Ishmael? They are the Arabs, who are proud to claim Ishmael as their father, and to consider themselves through him the children of Abraham. We know that God has greatly blessed them as he promised Abraham he would do. Many of them, like many of the children of Isaac, have believed on Christ and have become true children of Abraham (Rom. 4:11, 16-17).

However, most of the children of Ishmael have

not yet put their trust in Christ for salvation. The great majority of Arabs today are not Christians but Muslims. They followed Muhammad the "prophet of Arabia," of the seed of Ishmael, and the blessing of salvation which God promised to the world through Christ has not yet become theirs. Not only are millions of Arabs believers in Muhammad and the Koran, but hundreds of millions of people of non-Arab descent in Turkey and Iran and Pakistan and India and Indonesia and Africa and many other lands profess the faith of Islam. They, too, consider Abraham their spiritual father, and they honor Ishmael rather than Isaac. They believe that it was Ishmael, not Isaac, whom Abraham was about to sacrifice at God's command, when God supplied a ram in his place.

God, in answer to the prayer of Abraham, has blessed the descendants of Ishmael in many ways, and today has made them the custodians of much of the oil which he created in the earth. Is not their father Abraham awaiting in heaven the complete answer to his prayer that they will "live in God's sight," which is that the blessing of life eternal through Christ will be theirs? And may we not believe that this supreme blessing is intended not for the Arabs alone, but also for all the spiritual children of Ishmael? For God in love gave his only Son for the salvation of the *world,* and that includes the 800 million Muslims now living on the earth. As Peter reminds us, God does not wish "that any should perish, but that all should reach repentance" (II Pet. 3:9). Accordingly, Paul prayed for the children of Israel, and his "heart's desire" was that they be saved. As we learn from his letters and from the accounts of his labors, he had the same passionate desire for the salvation of the Gentiles also.

That divinely created longing for the salvation of all men which throbbed in the heart of Paul has been bestowed in lesser degree to a host of Christ's servants, who age after age in all parts of the world have sought to save the sheep that were lost. And on the hearts of some God laid the special burden of the salvation of the people of Islam, so that they could say with deep sincerity, "Our heart's desire is that Muslims may be saved." To this end they devoted their lives to prayer and labor for the salvation of the followers of Muhammad.

One of those whom God called to the task of evangelizing Muslims was Samuel M. Zwemer, who went from America as a pioneer missionary to Arabia in 1890, and the title of whose biography is *Apostle to Islam*.[1] The consuming passion of Zwemer's life was to make Christ known to Muslims. I first saw Samuel Zwemer at the great Convention of the Student Volunteer Movement for Foreign Missions at Kansas City in 1913. A gifted young man by the name of William Borden,[2] who had been studying Arabic in Cairo in preparation for going to China as a missionary to the millions of Muslims in that land, died in Egypt.

---

[1] J. Christy Wilson, Sr., *Apostle to Islam* (Baker Book House, 1952).

[2] Mrs. Howard Taylor, *Borden of Yale '09* (China Inland Mission, 1926).

Dr. Zwemer told us of Borden's death, and called for volunteers to go to China in his place.

Several years later Dr. Zwemer gave a series of lectures at Princeton Theological Seminary, where I was a student, and there brought powerfully to our attention the needs of the Muslim world. He told us that Islam was the only one of the great religions of the world which had come into existence after Christianity. It was the only one which claimed to have taken the place of Christianity as the one true religion of the world. Islam embraces one-sixth of the population of the world. Its adherents had been more neglected by missionaries of the gospel than any other people. And fewer converts to Christianity had been made from the followers of Muhammad than from those of any other great religion. Dr. Zwemer challenged the students of Princeton Seminary to go as missionaries to Muslims.

The fire in Dr. Zwemer's soul kindled a blaze in other hearts, and a number of us who listened to his appeal heard in it God's call to us to go to the Muslim world with the Good News of Christ. One who went to Iran was J. Christy Wilson, who became Zwemer's biographer. I volunteered to go to Meshed, a sacred city in northeast Iran, where a small group of Presbyterian missionaries had established a mission station and were carrying on medical and evangelistic work. It was their hope that they would be able to make Christ known both in the province of Khorasan (as large as France), in which there was no other Christian witness, and also in nearby Afghanistan. It was my privilege to share in the work of Christ in Iran from 1919 to 1962, when I retired.

Now in 1975 I can still say that my heart's desire is that Muslims may be saved and may know the love of Christ which passes knowledge. As I discuss in the pages of this little book the task to which God called me, and to which I have devoted many years of my life, I hope that God will use what is written to inspire others to say, "Our heart's desire and prayer to God for the Muslims is that they may be saved," and also to devote their lives to making known to the Muslims of the world the Good News of Jesus Christ.

2
How Islam Began

HOW ISLAM BEGAN

It is essential that those Christians who have the opportunity to tell the Good News of Christ to their Muslim friends and acquaintances, as well as those who desire to pray intelligently for Muslims and for those who by word and deed are making Christ known to them, should understand clearly who Muhammad was and what he taught. Though many excellent books have been written by Christian scholars about the history and teachings of Islam, it seems that some Christians have vague ideas about how this religio-political system began, and on what doctrines and practices it was established. In this chapter the most interesting story of the "Prophet of Arabia" will be briefly told as it was related by the early Muslim historians. A sincere effort will be made to "speak the truth in love" (Eph. 4:15). However, it is not possible to tell the story of Muhammad's life with complete historical accuracy, for the sources available consist largely of traditions, some of which originated long after the death of Muhammad. The source that is most reliable is the Koran. The facts stated in the following pages are those on which most of the Muslim and non-Muslim writers agree.

Arabia at the Time of Muhammad

In the providence of God a baby boy was born in Mecca, in the western part of Arabia, about the year A.D. 570, to whom the name Muhammad (meaning "Praised") was given. Little did those who named the child realize that he was destined to influence the world as few other individuals have done, and would indeed be praised by untold millions of people for centuries to come.

Arabia is a vast land, much of which is desert. In the desert regions the Bedouin nomads moved about with their flocks and herds, living in their black tents. There were also cities in which rich merchants carried on their trade, the chief of which was Mecca. Through Mecca passed the camel caravans carrying merchandise between the Yemen in the south and Syria in the north. Mecca was both an important commercial center and also a shrine city. In it from ancient times had been located the Ka'aba (meaning "Cube"), a cubical building which was known as the "House of Allah." There was a tradition that when this holy House was destroyed by a flood, Abraham and his son Ishmael rebuilt it. In the Arabic language "Allah" means "The God," and it seems that the Arabs recognized him as the Supreme God. Whether they learned of him from the Jews or inherited this knowledge from their ancestor Abraham, is not evident. The name of Muhammad's father was Abdullah, which means "slave of Allah."

Though the Arabs recognized Allah as supreme

they did not consider him to be the only god, nor did they place importance on his worship. They worshiped a number of other deities, and at the time of Muhammad's youth the Ka'aba was full of the images of other gods and godesses. When the Arabs came to Mecca to trade at the annual fairs, they also performed the customary rites of the pilgrimage to Ka'aba, walking around it seven times, and kissing or touching the Black Stone which was built into the wall. This was a meteorite to which great religious significance was attached. Though the Arabs were not a very religious people, the shrine at Mecca and its ritual were precious to them as an important element in their cultural heritage.

Hanifs, Jews, and Christians in Arabia

Not all the people of Mecca were satisfied with conditions in their country. The political situation was not good, for the many small tribes were frequently warring with one another, and because of their lack of unity were in danger of being swallowed up by the great empires about them, those of Persia and Byzantium and Ethiopia. The popular religion did not satisfy those few individuals who wanted to know God. It is said that a small group of intelligent men known as Hanifs used to meet together to discuss these political and religious problems.

Were there no people in Arabia who could tell them of the one true God? Yes, from ancient times large numbers of Jews had resided in

Arabia, and a few of them were in Mecca. In Madina, which was 280 miles north of Mecca, there were three large tribes of Jews, with their synagogues and their Scriptures. They had prospered materially; they owned camels and houses and lands, and largely controlled the commerce of the city. Their education and standard of living were higher than those of the pagan Arabs around them. The Arabs knew that the Jews did not worship idols, but were worshipers of Allah, the unseen God. But it is improbable that the Jews made known to the pagans the spiritual treasures which were in their Scriptures.

Also there were Christians in Arabia. In the north there were several Arab tribes which had become Christian. In the south in Nejran were many Christians who had their bishops and priests, and their Scriptures in the Syriac language. This Nestorian "Church of the East," which had previously sent its missionaries into Arabia, had not met with great success in its efforts to convert the Arabs, most of whom had remained pagans. It seems that the Christians lacked the love and purity of life and spiritual power needed to make them an effective missionary agency in Arabia.

Birth and Youth of Muhammad

Abdullah, the father of Muhammad, died before the birth of his son in Mecca about 570. Amina, Muhammad's mother, died when he was six years of age, and the orphaned boy was entrusted to the care of his grandfather. The old man soon died, and Muhammad was taken by his uncle, Abu Talib, who was kind to him. Muhammad's family was a part of the very powerful tribe called Quraish, which was responsible for the Ka'aba. But Abu Talib, though influential, was poor, and it is said that for a time Muhammad served as a shepherd in the desert. It is also said that when he was twelve years of age he accompanied his uncle, who went with a trading caravan to Syria.

Marriage and Growing Influence of Muhammad

The youth became a man of ability and good character. At the age of twenty-five he was employed by a wealthy widow in Mecca, named Khadijeh, to accompany her caravan to Syria. So successful was he in this business venture that on his return Khadijeh, who was forty years of age, made him an offer of marriage. Muhammad agreed, and his wife gave him love and wealth and an influential position in Meccan society. Two sons and four daughters were born to Muhammad and Khadijeh, and till her death twenty-five years later he took no other wife. To their great sorrow both sons died in infancy. During these years Muhammad associated with the chief people of Mecca, and became well acquainted with the religious and political situation in his country. Khadijeh was a relative of one of the Hanifs who had become a Christian, and it is probable that

Muhammad discussed with him and the other Hanifs the problems of Arabia. Muhammad knew that Jews and Christians worshiped Allah and did not worship images. Though he continued to worship at the Ka'aba, it is probable that he had begun to realize that the images in this House of Allah were no gods.

From what we know of the history of Muhammad it seems clear that he was a sincere seeker for God. He now had leisure and money for travel. Did it not occur to him that he could go to Nejran or Syria or Ethiopia to inquire from learned Christians what their Scriptures taught about God? It seems that Muhammad never made a serious effort to learn what was written in the Scriptures which he knew were in the hands of Jews and Christians, and which he later attested as being true. The accounts which came to him of the contents of the Bible were evidently from people who were unable or unwilling to give him correct information. As a result, to the end of his life Muhammad never learned what the true gospel is. Was he prevented from going to Christian teachers by what he saw of the bitter quarrels among members of the different branches of the Church? Did his national pride in being an Arab from Mecca make him unwilling to humble himself and go to Jews or Christians, minority peoples, for guidance? Whatever the cause may have been, it is probable that it was at this point that Muhammad missed the way to God. He failed to seek spiritual help from those qualified to show him Christ, the Way to the Father.

Muhammad's Appointment to Be the Prophet of Allah

It is said that Muhammad and other seekers for God used to go from time to time to a cave three miles from Mecca to meditate and worship. One night in the month of Ramadan, about the year 610, when Muhammad was forty years of age, he and his family were at this cave. According to tradition, the angel Gabriel came to Muhammad as he slept and commanded him to recite. The command was twice repeated, and Muhammad asked what he was to recite. The angel replied, "Recite thou in the name of the Lord, who created man from clots of blood" (Koran, Sura 96). When he awoke Muhammad was in great doubt as to what this experience meant. Was it from the jinn, the creatures who inspired the soothsayers, or was it from Allah? Muhammad had heard from the Jews of the prophets whom Allah had sent to the people of Israel. But no prophet had ever been sent to the Arabs. Could this be a message from Allah that he was to be a prophet and apostle to his own people? He confided in his faithful wife, and she comforted him and assured him that this was indeed an appointment to the prophetic office. However, it seems that for some months, during which time no more revelations came to him, Muhammad was deeply depressed, and even considered suicide.

After about two years other revelations began to come in various forms. Sometimes Muhammad saw the angel Gabriel, sometimes he only heard a voice, and sometimes he heard the sound of a bell through which the words of the angel were brought to him. Sometimes the message came in a dream, and at other times it came in the thoughts of his mind. When revelation came to him his whole frame would become agitated, and perspiration would pour down his face. He would often fall to the ground and foam at the mouth. The messages always came to him in the Arabic language, and Muhammad spoke the words that he received, and they were written down by people who heard them from Muhammad's lips. It is generally supposed by Muslims that Muhammad was himself illiterate. After his death these messages were collected and incorporated in the Koran (the Arabic is Qur'an, which means "recitation"). Muhammad was convinced that the words which came to him were not his own, but the very Word of God, and he was only the "reciter." Thus Muslims believe that the Koran is not Muhammad's book, but God's.

The Message Which Came to Muhammad

The heart of the message which Muhammad received was that there is no god but Allah, the one true God, who created heaven and earth and everything in them. Man is God's slave, and it is his first duty to submit to God and obey him. God's goodness and mercy are seen in his provision for all the needs of men, and men must be grateful. A great and terrible day is coming, when the earth will be shaken, and God will raise all the dead to life, and will judge them. He will reward with the pleasures of a sensual paradise those who worship him and do good deeds, and will condemn to the fires of hell those who do evil deeds, the worst of which is associating other gods with God. Whence did Muhammad derive this message? Muslims insist that it came to him by direct revelation from God. We may surmise however, that the truth of the oneness of God had been impressed on his mind by his contacts with the Jews. And possibly the expectation of the resurrection and final judgment, a doctrine repugnant to the materialistic Arabs, had come to Muhammad from the preaching of some Christian missionary. In whatever way these truths came to him, Muhammad proclaimed them with great earnestness, seeking to bring the people of Mecca to repentance and faith in one God.

The Effects of Muhammad's Preaching in Mecca

When Muhammad made the claim that he was a prophet sent by God, there were a few people who at once believed on him. They were his wife Khadijeh, a young cousin Ali, who was a member of his family, and his adopted son Zaid. Then an honorable merchant, later known as Abu Bakr, who was not a relative, professed faith in Muhammad. And others, most of them people of humble origin, joined the movement. But the leading people of the city, whom Muhammad was eager to win, ignored and soon began to ridicule him. Who was he, a common man, to make such

21

a claim for himself? And his message about the resurrection was incredible. How could dead bones come to life again? They accused him of sorcery and fraud. As Muhammad began to attack the gods in the Ka'aba, saying they were no gods, the men of Mecca became increasingly angry and began to persecute his little band of a hundred followers. They could do nothing to Muhammad, because he was protected by his uncle Abu Talib.

The persecution became so severe that Muhammad sent eighty of his followers to Ethiopia, a Christian country. They were well treated there, till they later joined Muhammad in Madina. The opposition did not stop Muhammad's bitter denunciation of his enemies, whom he threatened with the wrath of God. New converts joined him, and he encouraged them to be strong by telling them stories of the courage of the ancient prophets and believers in times of suffering.

Progress in the Formation of the Muslim Community

During these years Muhammad was engaged in building up a community of people bound together not by blood ties, as in Arab society, but by faith in Allah and his Apostle. Their basic belief, which later became their creed, was, "There is no god but Allah, Muhammad is the Apostle of Allah." Those who submitted in faith to Allah and his Apostle were known as "Muslims," since in Arabic *muslim* (or moslem) means "one who submits." From the same Arabic root comes *Is-lam,* which means "submission." This became the name by which the movement was known. Islam was from the first conceived to be a "church-state," a religio-political society, in which Muhammad was under God the ruler in matters both religious and civil. His position resembled that of Moses in the theocracy of Israel. The Quraish in Mecca realized that a state within their state was being created, and they deeply resented its presence.

In the tenth year of his mission (620) Muhammad suffered two great losses. His uncle Abu Talib died, the kind man who had helped him and protected him from his childhood, though he never became a Muslim. Also Khadijeh, his faithful and able wife, died. After a few months Muhammad sought comfort by marrying the widow of one of the believers. He also married Ayisha, the seven-year-old daughter of his friend Abu Bakr, whom he took to his abode three years later. She became his favorite wife.

The Decision to Move to Madina

Being unable to make further progress in Mecca, Muhammad saw no alternative to a transfer of his mission to a more favorable location. He decided to go to Yathrib, a city 280 miles north of Mecca, which after his going there became known as Madina ("The City of the Prophet"). The people of Yathrib were more openminded than were the keepers of the Ka'aba, and about half of the inhabitants of that region were Jews. The pagan Arabs looked up to the Jews for their superior culture and wealth, but resented their economic success. It is said that in 621 Muhammad met twelve men from Madina who had come to Mecca for the annual pilgrimage and converted them to Islam. They made more converts in their city, and at the pilgrimage a year later seventy-two men and two women from Madina met Muhammad and swore allegiance to him, promising to defend him with their lives. He also promised to fight for them. From this alliance we see the nature of the society which Muhammad wanted to establish.

As the time of departure approached, Muhammad had a vision which must have cheered him as he contemplated his thirteen years of unsuccessful effort to win the people of his native city to his side. He saw himself carried from Mecca to Jerusalem, the city which he and his followers faced in their worship, as did the Jews. From Jerusalem he was carried up into heaven, where he talked with apostles and prophets of the past, and was attested and honored by them. In some of the traditions this "Night Journey" is related as a bodily ascension to heaven. But in another tradition his wife Ayisha stated that on that night Muhammad did not leave his bed. The courage and faith of Muhammad during these years of comparative failure in Mecca, and his assurance of final victory, are indeed worthy of praise. Would that he had thus endured in the service of Jesus Christ!

The Hegira or Migration to Madina in A.D. 622

In his final message to the people of Mecca Muhammad sternly denounced them for their unbelief and threatened them with terrible punishment, both in this world and also in the next. He then bade his followers make their way in small parties to Madina, a journey of several weeks by camel. Learning that the Quraish were planning to prevent him from departing, he and Abu Bakr escaped from the city, hid for several days in a cave, and then by a safe route made their way to Madina. This migration, called in Arabic *Hijra,* took place in the summer of 622. From this event Muslims date their history, since it is thought that Islam truly began when the Prophet and his followers established their community in Madina. Today in Muslim lands documents, letters, newspapers, etc., are dated from the *Hijra.*

During his years in Mecca Muhammad never claimed that he had performed a miracle to prove that he was a prophet. However, when asked what sign he could show to convince the people that God had sent him, he replied that his miracle was the Koran, the verses of which are called "signs" in Arabic, because no one was able to produce the like of it. Muhammad considered the Scriptures of the Jews and Christians to be true, but he thought the followers of these religions had misinterpreted them and had corrupted their religions. He maintained that God had sent him to call people back to the true worship of God, which was the religion of Abraham. In leading his followers in worship he imitated the Jews in facing Jerusalem, and he was eager to win the allegiance and support of the Jews. He never claimed divinity for himself, and said to the people, "I am a man like you." He was aware that he needed to confess his sins and ask pardon of God as did other men.

Muhammad in Madina

When Muhammad rode into Madina on his camel many people of different tribes urged him to become their guest. Not wishing to offend any of them by a refusal, he allowed his camel to decide for him. When the camel sat down of its own accord to permit its rider to dismount, there Muhammad established his residence and built the first mosque ever built for worship. It is said that his first sermon was preached on a Friday, with the result that Friday became the day for congregational worship in Islam. Zaid was sent back to Mecca to bring the family of Muhammad to their new home. The political situation in Madina was confused, as there was no central authority to keep the peace among the various tribes. Soon Muhammad was able to become the civil as well as the religious ruler in the city, as more and more people submitted to him and became Muslims. It seems that he ruled wisely and brought law and order to his new capital.

Muhammad at first looked to the Jews in Madina to attest and support his claims. It was probably at this time that a revelation came to him directing him to take a conciliatory attitude toward people who had not believed on him, and not to use force to induce them to accept Islam. The command was: "Let there be no compulsion in religion" (Sura 2:257). Later this verse was abrogated. Though some of the Jews assured Muhammad that his coming had been predicted in their Scriptures, which was the attestation he sought, most of them remained aloof. They knew he could not be their Messiah, who must be of the family of David. When Muhammad detected their attitude he called them hypocrites. They then told him frankly that his coming was not foretold in their Scriptures, and he replied by accusing them of misinterpreting their sacred books. He did not charge them with changing the text of the Scriptures, but of omitting the references to him.

In the second year of the Hegira the break with the Jews became complete. He had at first observed their holy Day of Atonement, but now instituted in its place the Ramadan month of fasting. He also instituted the Feast of Sacrifice in memory of Abraham's sacrificing the ram instead of his son. Till now he and his followers had faced north toward Jerusalem in their worship, but a revelation came to him to change the prayer direction to Mecca. It is said that one day as he was standing in front of the believers in the mosque, leading in their prayers facing Jerusalem, he suddenly turned about toward the south, and completed the worship facing Mecca. Having failed to win the Jews, he sought in this way to win the favor of the Quraish. Muhammad justified this radical change by saying that the Ka'aba had been dedicated by Abraham and was the original center for the worship of God. This turnabout in worship was an act of very great significance, for it indicated an abandonment of the Jewish-Christian tradition, and the launching forth on a new course which was related to, but in many essentials in conflict with, the teachings of the Bible. Islam had now been established as an independent religio-political system.

The Decision to Use Force

During the second year in Madina life became very difficult for the immigrants from Mecca. Their funds were exhausted, and probably the hospitality of the believers from Madina was being strained. Something must be done if the community was to continue. What solution was provided by Allah? This revelation came to Muhammad: "O Prophet, contend against the infidels and be rigorous with them" (Sura 9:74). So Muhammad began to do what Bedouin chieftains usually did when in financial difficulties—he began with divine approval to raid the caravans of his enemies in Mecca. He had tried for thirteen years by peaceful means to induce them to submit to him, and had failed. Now he would use the sword, and by capturing their caravans he would both hurt them and help himself.

Accordingly, Muhammad sent out a party in

the "sacred months," during which it was the custom of the Arabs to refrain from warfare, to capture a caravan belonging to Mecca. They met with success, and divided the booty. The violation of the "sacred months" was justified by a revelation that came to Muhammad.

Encouraged by this victory, an attempt was made to capture a very large caravan which was about to return from Syria laden with merchandise. Muhammad went forth in person with 350 armed men, and at a place called Badr met and defeated the army of 1,000 men that had come from Mecca to protect the caravan. It is said that 49 men in the army from Mecca were killed, while Muhammad lost 14 of his followers. The booty was divided among the warriors, and one-fifth was kept by Muhammad, to be used by him in helping the needy. This became a precedent for the division of the spoils of war. The victory at Badr was of very great importance for Islam. It assured Muhammad that God was with him. It convinced his followers that they were on the winning side, and would profit from future victories. It alarmed the Quraish, who began to fear that they would finally be defeated by Muhammad. It also induced many pagan Arabs to come to Madina and submit to Muhammad as their ruler. And it indicated that the sword was more effective than the tongue in making converts for Islam.

Attacks on the Jews of Madina

The Jews were unhappy over Muhammad's victory at Badr, and some of them composed and recited verses in which they ridiculed the people of Madina for submitting to a man who had slain his own people in battle. The Muslim historians tell of at least four Jews, one of whom was a woman, who were assassinated by the zealous followers of Muhammad for this crime. The assassins were not even rebuked by Muhammad for what they had done.

Realizing that the Jews were his enemies, Muhammad determined to get rid of them. He accused one of the tribes, called Banu Qainuqa, of breaking a treaty, and informed them they must accept Islam. When they refused, the Muslims besieged them for fifteen days, defeated them, and drove them from their homes, and confiscated all their property.

Soon after this an army of a thousand men came up from Mecca for the purpose of defeating Muhammad. They met the Muslim army at a place near Madina called Uhud, and there inflicted a defeat on them, and Muhammad was himself wounded. But for some reason the Meccans did not follow up their victory, and went back home. This defeat was a humiliation for Muhammad, and he was comforted by revelations which came to him, explaining that the fault was with the Muslim soldiers who had disobeyed orders, and the defeat was permitted by God to test their faith. Final victory was promised, and Muhammad was able to encourage his followers to endure their sufferings, and their sorrow in the loss of many who fell in the battle.

Having fought and defeated several hostile

tribes, Muhammad next attacked another Jewish tribe, the Banu Nadir, which had been friendly to some of his enemies. They were ordered to leave all their possessions and depart. On their refusal to do so, a force of Muslims was sent against them, which cut down their date trees and ruined their properties. Seeing they could resist no longer they agreed to depart, and were allowed to take with them only what they could carry on their camels. Their arms and their crops were divided among the Muslims.

After a time Muhammad attacked another large Jewish tribe called the Banu Quraiza, which to this time had been friendly to him, but had recently failed to participate in one of his battles. Tradition states that Gabriel came to Muhammad and ordered him to arise and strike "the idolaters who are possessors of the Book, the Banu Quraiza." At once a large force was sent against this tribe. When their provisions were exhausted and they were unable to resist any longer they asked permission to emigrate as the Banu Nadir had done. This request was refused, and they were ordered to surrender unconditionally. This they were forced to do. Then the women and children were sold into slavery, their property was divided among the Muslim soldiers, and their 800 men were taken to Madina and there massacred. Thus the Jews in and about Madina were eliminated.

The Wives of Muhammad

After the death of Khadijeh Muhammad took

one wife after another. After he had married his sixth wife he desired to marry Zainab, the beautiful wife of Zaid, his adopted son. According to Arab custom it was unlawful for a man to marry the wife of an adopted son, even if her husband divorced her. However, a revelation came to Muhammad that God had permitted him to have Zainab, whereupon Zaid divorced her and she became Muhammad's seventh wife. At the time of his death, according to Muslim historians, Muhammad had twelve wives and two concubines, one of whom was Mary, a Coptic Christian slave who had been given to Muhammad by the ruler of Egypt. Each of his wives had a separate room, and Muhammad slept in their rooms in turn. It is not surprising that peace did not always prevail in the Prophet's household.

The Final Struggle with Mecca

In the fifth year of the Hegira the Quraish made a final desperate attempt to destroy Muhammad and his rule in Madina. They approached Madina with an army of 10,000 men. The Muslims dug a trench about the city to defend it, and the Meccans were unable to break through and take the city. When their provisions were exhausted they returned to Mecca, and never again attempted to fight Muhammad.

But Muhammad was determined to subdue Mecca, the one place in Arabia which he most desired to possess. He longed to make the Pilgrimage once more to the House of Allah, and so in 628 he and a group of Muslim pilgrims travelled toward Mecca. However, the Quraish refused them entrance into the city. Then negotiations were carried on with the Quraish, and a treaty was made in which both sides agreed not to fight for ten years, and permission was granted for Muhammad and his followers to enter Mecca unarmed the following year. The followers of the Prophet thought they had met with defeat, but Muhammad assured them it was a great victory. A revelation came stating that Islam, the religion of truth, will be "exalted above every religion" (Sura 48:27-28). Henceforth Judaism and Christianity are to be superseded by Islam.

After winning other victories over rebel tribes, Muhammad and 2,000 of his followers in 629 took advantage of the permission granted them in the treaty and came to Mecca for the Lesser Pilgrimage. On their approach the Quraish vacated the city, and the Muslims entered unarmed. Muhammad performed all the rites of the pagan ritual, going seven times about the Ka'aba, which was still full of images, and kissing the Black Stone, and offering the sacrifices. He also married his eleventh wife, and won to his side several of his former foes.

Though it had been agreed that there would be no more war for ten years, Muhammad was convinced that he must now conquer Mecca, in order to make his control of Arabia complete. And so as soon as he returned to Madina from the Lesser Pilgrimage he raised an army of 10,000 men and started back to Mecca. When he reached the city Abu Sufyan, the leader of the Quraish and one of the bitterest of the foes of Muhammad, realizing that further resistance was useless, came out to meet the conqueror and became a Muslim. The army entered the city unopposed. Muhammad went to the Ka'aba and ordered that the images be brought out and destroyed. He took over the rule of the city, from which he had fled eight years before. He declared a general amnesty to the people of Mecca, with the exception of a few individuals who were executed for certain crimes. Mecca now became the center of Islam, with Muhammad as its supreme ruler. It was indeed a day of triumph and great joy for Muhammad and his followers. The new believers in Mecca were rewarded for their submission by being given generous portions of the large booty recently taken in a victory at Hunain over some rebel tribes. But some of the old believers were not happy about this.

Conversion by Force Commanded

During the ninth year of the Hegira many tribes, realizing that they could no longer resist Muhammad, came and submitted to him. At this time a revelation came which abrogated the previous command not to use force in making converts (Sura 2:257). It was this: "When the sacred months are past, kill those who join other gods with God wherever ye shall find them, and seize them, besiege them, and lay wait for them with every kind of ambush; but if they shall convert and observe prayer and pay the obligatory alms let them go their way" (Sura 9:5). The purpose of this command was to put an end to idolatry, and it was outwardly, at least, highly successful. Not only were pagans forced at the point of the sword to become Muslims, a Christian prince in the north of Arabia named Ukaider was promised his life if he accepted Islam. This he did. From this we would infer that Christians, because of their worship of Christ, were at this time counted as polytheists.

However, a different policy was adopted toward the Christians of Nejran in the south of Arabia. Tradition states that when a lettter from Muhammad commanding them to become Muslims reached this large Christian community, they were greatly perplexed as to what they should do. Should they submit, or should they fight Muhammad? It was decided that they would send a large deputation to talk with him. Their bishop and a number of their chief men made the long journey to Madina. They found Muhammad in the mosque, and he welcomed them and permitted them to perform their Christian worship there. After three days Muhammad invited them to accept Islam. A discussion followed about *Isa* (Jesus), in which Muhammad said Jesus was his brother, and was only a servant of God, by whose permission he had healed the sick and raised the dead to life. But the Christians insisted that Jesus was God's Son, and refused to give up their faith in him and become Muslims.

At this point a revelation came to Muhammad,

instructing him to challenge the Christians to trial by imprecation. They would curse one another, and let God decide who was right and who wrong. So Muhammad went out with his daughter Fatima and her husband Ali and their sons Hasan and Husayn, and sat under a cloak. The Christians came to meet them adorned in the finest silken garments. Being deeply impressed by the simplicity of the Holy Family of Islam, and fearful of being destroyed by the curse of Muhammad, they refused to participate in the trial. So relates the Islamic tradition. We do not have the account the Christians gave of this remarkable confrontation.

It is said that Muhammad permitted these Christians to keep their religion and be under his protection, provided they paid a high tribute. These terms they accepted, and returned to their homes. This was probably the first time that Muhammad had come face to face with educated and influential Christians. However, it seems that he made no effort to learn from them the true teachings of their religion, and only wished to subdue them. In this he succeeded.

Farewell Pilgrimage and Death of Muhammad (632)

In the tenth year of the Hegira Muhammad went to Mecca for the Greater Pilgrimage, which was his last. He took with him all his wives, and it is said that a hundred thousand people accompanied him. He performed all the rites of the

Pilgrimage according to the ancient pagan customs, thus incorporating them into his religion and setting an example for all future pilgrims. He there delivered an address in which he said, "This day I have perfected your religion for you" (Sura 5:5).

The Muslims of the Shi'ite sect have a tradition that on the return journey to Madina Muhammad halted the caravan in a very hot place in the desert and assembled the people about him. Then he called his son-in-law Ali to his side and appointed him as his successor, and bade the people obey him. This tradition is rejected by other Muslims as untrue.

Not long after the return of Muhammad to Madina he became very ill. Fearing that after his death his followers might quarrel among themselves, he admonished the leaders to be loyal to one another and to obey his successor. He directed Abu Bakr to lead the worship when he was too ill to do so, and it was thought by some that this was an indication that he should succeed Muhammad. Finally, on June 8, 632, death came to Muhammad in the room of Ayisha as he rested on her lap. It is said that a grave was dug in that very place, and in it the Prophet of Arabia was buried. Later a mosque was built, and the grave became a place of pilgrimage.

Events That Followed
the Death of Muhammad

As soon as Muhammad died a power struggle

took place. If Ali had really been appointed by Muhammad as successor, he was not chosen to that position by the leaders, for they finally gave their allegiance to Abu Bakr. He became the first caliph (vicegerent). Three others followed, the fourth being Ali. The three were all assassinated by other Muslims. Wars followed, Muslims slaying other Muslims. However, in spite of these serious internal difficulties, the Muslim armies went forth to conquer the world. They met with amazing success, which they believed was proof that God was with them.

In a short time the Muslim armies, fired by religious zeal and eager for plunder and conquest, defeated the armies of the Persian and Byzantine empires. They conquered Syria and Egypt, moved across North Africa conquering lands which had been strongly Christian, and occupied Spain. Only in 732 was their westward advance stopped by Charles Martel in the battle of Tours in France. Eastward also they went, conquering all the lands to the Oxus and Indus rivers. Islam continued to advance, by peaceful means or by warfare, till it was established all across Asia and Africa. Now one-seventh of the population of the world are proud to be called Muslims.

Conclusion

We have attempted to tell accurately and fairly the story of Muhammad, the founder of Islam. What is to be our estimate of him? Every possible opinion about him has been expressed. He has been pictured as God's most perfect and holy prophet. He has also been considered a devil incarnate, who, according to Dante, is to be the chief among the damned because he led many people astray. That he was a man of great ability, who achieved remarkable success in the face of almost insuperable difficulties, cannot be questioned. As a leader he had the outstanding ability to win and hold the allegiance of men. He was a very religious man who hated idols and was passionately devoted to Allah, whom he considered to be the one true God. His courage and perseverance in proclaiming the doctrine of the unity of God are indeed inspiring.

However, when the life of this great man is measured by the standard of Jesus Christ, he is found wanting. It seems that he began his mission as a sincere and obedient proclaimer of the truth as he saw it. But somewhere in his life he lost his way. Having failed to inquire about the way to God from those qualified to guide him, he took the wrong road, which led him and untold multitudes who followed him far from the truth. By ignoring the teachings of Christ, either intentionally or through ignorance, Muhammad never knew how much God loved him and all mankind in giving his Son to save the world.

Not knowing God truly, Muhammad began to place political expedience and even personal preferences above the moral and ethical principles which he had taught. It appears that he used the revelations which he said came from God to justify actions which even the pagan Arabs considered wrong. And in claiming that Islam had taken the place of Christianity, and that he as the "Seal of the Prophets" had supplanted Christ, he rejected God's holy purpose for the salvation of the world through Christ alone. The message of every true prophet of God must be in agreement with the messages of the prophets who preceded him. Since the message of Muhammad is in many important respects contradictory to the Word of God revealed by previous prophets and apostles, and particularly to the truth of Jesus Christ, it is not possible for Christians to consider Muhammad to have been God's prophet. Rather he is one of those foretold by Christ in Matthew 24: 24-25, who would lead many astray. It is for their salvation that we must labor and pray.

3

Beliefs and Practices of Muslims

BELIEFS AND PRACTICES
OF MUSLIMS

It is not possible for a Christian to present the truths of the gospel to Muslims effectively unless he is acquainted with the doctrines and duties inculcated by Islam. In Islam as in Christianity there are many different sects and many schools of thought, but all agree in the creed which makes them Muslims: "There is no god but God, Muhammad is God's Apostle." Most of them also agree in certain basic doctrines and obligatory duties of their religion. In the preceding chapter many of the doctrines stated in the Koran were mentioned. In this chapter these doctrines and practices as they were later developed by Muslim theologians will be discussed, in the order in which they are treated in Muslim creeds.

Belief in God (Allah)

The pagan Arabs at the time of Muhammad worshiped many gods and goddesses, the images of whom were in the Ka'aba in Mecca. They knew that there was a supreme God, whom they called "Allah" (The God), who was Lord of the Ka'aba, but they were more attached to the other gods than to him. Muhammad proclaimed that

Allah alone was God, and that the others were only idols which should not be worshiped. This became the basic belief of Islam, that God is One, and that attributing partners to God is the greatest sin one can commit. Hence the idolatry practiced in India and other lands is abhorrent to Muslims.

Muslim theologians have stated that the unity of God implies that he is different from anything that man can conceive. Hence God's being is defined in negatives—he is not body or spirit or substance or attribute, he does not have parts or members, and he cannot be seen. However, in the Koran there is much that is positive about the character of God. He is the Creator of all things. He sustains the universe by his power, and nothing happens without his will. He created man to be his slave, and requires from men obedience and worship. God will raise all the dead to life and will judge them. In mercy he has sent prophets to warn men and to guide them in the right way. He is forgiving and will pardon whom he will. He does whatever he wills to do, and it is not for men to question him. The attributes usually attributed to God are the following: life, knowledge, will, power, hearing, seeing, and speaking. In the Koran and the traditions are terms which have been called the "Ninety-Nine Most Beautiful Names of God," some of which are the following: The One, The Real, The Light, The Self-Sustaining, The Eternal, The Avenger, The Judge. All the Suras of the Koran, with one exception, begin with the words: "In the Name of God, the Compassionate, the Merciful." The theologians explain that when these qualities are attributed to God they have a different meaning than when used of men.

As the theme of God dominates the Koran, so the mention of the name of God dominates the speech of many Muslims. When one promises to do something he conditions his agreement by saying, "If God wills." When he sneezes he is to say, "Praise God!" At the sight of something beautiful he should say, "Glory to God!" In all circumstances he is taught to say, "Thanks be to God!" When the donkey driver wants to hasten the pace of his weary beast he calls out, "Ya Allah!" (O God!). If the love of God were in the hearts of Muslims as much as his name is on their lips, they would indeed be a most godly people. It is the boast of Muslims that they are monotheists and believe in only the one true God. But is this enough? In his Epistle James writes: "You believe that God is one; you do well. Even the demons believe—and shudder" (James 2:19).

Belief in God's Angels

Muslims believe that God created hosts of angels, all of whom are sinless. They do not eat or drink, and are sexless. They will finally die, and be raised in the resurrection. The pagan Arabs thought that some of the angels were the "daughters of Allah," and this error was sternly rejected in the Koran. Angels are of various ranks. Four (or eight) bear up the throne of God. They are continually engaged in praising God and doing his will. They watch over believers, and intercede for them. Many thousands of angels aided the Muslims at the battle of Badr and gave them the victory. They take the souls of believers at death, and they also cause the death of sinners. Nineteen angels guard the gates of hell. Two fierce black angels visit corpses in the grave shortly after burial, and ask them, "Who is thy Lord? What is thy religion? Who is thy Prophet?" This imminent questioning is terrifying to those about to die.

Muslim traditions name the four archangels, who are: Gabriel, Michael, Izrail the Angel of Death, and Israfil, who will blow the trumpet on the last day to awake the dead. Gabriel is God's chief messenger, and in the Koran is referred to as the "Holy Spirit" and the "Illustrious Messenger endued with power." Since God is too exalted to speak directly to men, God's messages were brought to Muhammad by Gabriel. It was also Gabriel who appeared to the Virgin Mary and announced to her that she would have a son (Sura 19:17).

It is stated several times in the Koran that when God created Adam he commanded the angels to worship him. All did so except Iblis (diabolos, Satan), who refused, saying, "He was made of clay, but I was made of fire. I am better than he, so why should I worship him?" God cursed Iblis for his disobedience and cast him out of paradise, and he became man's chief enemy. He is the head of all the demons and evil jinn.

Belief in God's Prophets

Muslims believe that God in mercy sent many

prophets to all the nations of the world to guide erring men in the right way, and to convey his Word to them. Some Muslim sects have given the number of prophets as 124,000, others as 144,000. In the Koran the names of twenty-eight prophets are found, most of whom are biblical characters. The Great Prophets are said to be Adam, Noah, Abraham, Moses, Jesus, and Muhammad. Each of these was sent by God as his representative to all the people of the world for a long period of time. Each was given a Book by God containing laws both civil and religious for the regulating of the life of men. The laws given by one Prophet were in effect till they were abrogated by the laws contained in the Book brought from God by the succeeding Prophet. Each of the Great Prophets foretold the coming of the Prophet who would succeed him. The last and greatest of the Prophets is Muhammad, the "Seal of the Prophets" (Sura 33:40). No other prophet will come before the Day of Resurrection.

The prophets are not divine beings, but are "supermen." They are not to be worshiped. Though the Koran refers to the sins of the prophets (with the exception of Jesus), Muslims generally believe that all of God's prophets were sinless. For, they say, how can a sinner guide other sinners? It is believed that God gave books not only to the Great Prophets but also to a number of other prophets. These books were God's Word, but since the Koran has taken the place of all previous revelations of God's will, the laws in these books are not necessary or binding on men today. The Koran is all-sufficient.

The Koran in Sura 7 relates how God created Adam and Eve and placed them in the Garden. For their disobedience in eating the forbidden fruit, which tradition says was wheat, they were expelled from the Garden. However, since it is thought that prophets do not sin, it is said that Adam was not guilty of sinning, but "left the higher way." He repented, and God forgave him. After Adam God sent prophet after prophet to teach and warn men, most of whom were rejected by the people to whom they were sent. The Koran contains many stories of Abraham, Joseph, Moses, and other Old Testament characters, also of Zechariah and John the Baptist and Jesus. Some accounts agree fairly well with the biblical narrative, and some do not. It seems that Muhammad heard many stories from Jews and a few from Christians, some of which were from the Bible and some from traditions. The knowledge which Muslims have of the biblical prophets is therefore inadequate and in many instances is quite incorrect.

Muslims consider Jesus to be a very great prophet, in fact, the greatest of the Great Prophets with the exception of Muhammad, who took his place. The Koran tells of the birth of Jesus from the Virgin Mary, and of his miracles in childhood and after he became the Apostle of God. It states that he healed the sick, cleansed lepers, gave sight to the blind, raised the dead to life, and brought down from heaven a table furnished with food, though no detailed accounts are given of these miracles (Sura 5:110, 116). Jesus in the Koran is called the "Messiah," the "Word of God," and a "Spirit from God." The title by which Muslims often refer to him is "Spirit of God." But he must not be called "Son of God," a term generally understood in a physical sense, and he must not be worshiped as a god (Sura 4:169). There is no suggestion in the Koran that Jesus ever sinned or asked for God's forgiveness, as did other prophets. The Koran says that Jesus "will be illustrious in this world and in the next, and one of those who have near access to God" (Sura 3:40). No other prophet, not even Muhammad, is praised as highly in the Koran as is Jesus Christ.

It is in a misdirected effort to honor Jesus that the Koran states emphatically that the Jews did not crucify him. They are rebuked for saying: "Verily we have slain the Messiah, Jesus the son of Mary, an apostle of God." Then the Koran continues: "Yet they slew him not, and they crucified him not, but they had only his likeness" (Sura 4:156). The usual interpretation of this verse is that when Jesus' enemies were about to crucify him, God mercifully performed a miracle and delivered him from their hands. He caused someone else (perhaps Judas) to look like Jesus, and this person was crucified by mistake in Jesus' place. Jesus was taken by God to heaven, where he is alive today, and from whence he will come again to earth.

Also the Koran states that Jesus announced the

coming of an apostle whose name will be Ahmad (Sura 61:6). This is understood to be a prediction of the coming of Muhammad, the two words being derived from the same Arabic root. Hence Muslims assert that in believing on Muhammad they have been obedient to the command of Jesus to accept Muhammad, but Christians have not.

To the Muslims of the world Muhammad is the supreme personality, though in the Koran it is stated that he is only a man like other men (Sura 18:110). Some writers have said that the first thing which God created was the "Light of Muhammad," and everything else was created for him. The Muslim mystic Hallaj wrote: "All the Lights of the Prophets proceeded from his Light; he was before all, his name the first in the Book of Fate; he was known before all things and all being, and will endure after the end of all. All knowledge is a drop from his ocean, all wisdom a handful from his stream, all things an hour from his life."

Muhammad is thought to be the "Perfect Man," a sinless being, whose example should be followed in everything—in eating, in the care of hair and beard, in marriage and the treatment of wives, in one's relation to friends and enemies, in worship, in government and in war. Thus the example of Muhammad, as he is portrayed correctly or incorrectly in the Koran and the traditions, has profoundly influenced the lives of countless millions of Muslims, and is doing so today. A stream does not rise higher than its source. While some Muslims have attained a character holier and lovelier than that of their Prophet, it would seem that most of those who imitate Muhammad fail to reach even his level of moral and spiritual life.

As the name of Allah is constantly on the lips of his servants, so is the name of his Apostle. As one writer has said, "One hears this name in the bazaar and in the street, in the mosque and from the minaret, sailors sing it while hoisting their sails, coolies groan it to raise a burden, the beggar howls it to obtain alms; it is the cry of the faithful in attack, hushes babies to sleep as a cradle song, it is the pillow of the sick, the last word of the dying; it is written on the doorpost and in the hearts, as well as, since eternity, on the throne of God; the best name to give a child, the best to swear by for an end of all disputes." Such is the place of Muhammad in the lives of his followers round the world today.

Belief in the Books of God

Islam is a religion of revelation. God has spoken, and has given his Word to his prophets, to some of whom he has given also Books. It is said that the number of books given to the prophets is 104. In the Koran there are references to the *Torat* (of Moses), the *Suhuf* (sheets or books of the prophets), *Zabur* (Psalms of David), *Injil* (Gospel of Jesus), and *Quran* (Koran of Muhammad). It is supposed that Adam, Noah, Abraham, and other prophets had books which are now nonexistent. All of these books are the Word of God, and the teaching of all is basically the same. However, when God gives a new book to one of the Great Prophets he thereby abrogates the previous books. For the present age the Koran is alone adequate, and after the coming of Muhammad only its commands are binding on believers.

The Koran is not the word of Muhammad but the very Word of God. It was written from eternity on the "Preserved Tablet" in heaven, and was brought down portion by portion to Muhammad by the angel Gabriel during a period of twenty-two years. It was spoken by Muhammad, was written down by those who heard it, and was finally collected into a book, which is a little larger than the New Testament. For some years after the death of Muhammad there was great confusion as to what material of all that had been preserved should be included in the Koran. Finally in the caliphate of Uthman (644–656) one text was given official approval, and all other material was destroyed.

Since it is believed that the Koran was brought from heaven in its original Arabic form, this language is considered an essential part of it. It cannot, therefore, be translated like other books, and till recently Muslims have been reluctant to publish translations of their Holy Book for the hundreds of millions of believers who do not know Arabic. In a translation the Koran is a difficult book to read, lacking continuity and abounding in repetition. However, when read aloud in Arabic by a good reader, in a mosque or on the radio, it makes a tremendous impression on those who listen, even when they do not fully understand the meaning. Muslims consider the Koran to be the unique miracle of their Prophet, since no one has been able to produce the equal of it. Believers treat their copies of the Koran with reverence, often keeping them wrapped in beautiful covers, and never placing anything on top of them.

Even in a translation, the opening Sura of the Koran, which is called *Fatiheh,* is very impressive. In Arberry's translation it is as follows:

> In the Name of God, The Merciful, The
> Compassionate.
> Praise belongs to God, the Lord of all Being,
> The All-merciful, the All-compassionate,
> The Master of the Day of Doom.
> Thee only we serve, to Thee alone we pray
> for succor.
> Guide us in the straight path,
> the path of those whom Thou has blessed,
> not of those against whom Thou art
> wrathful,
> nor of those who are astray.

The Shi'ite Belief in the Imams

There are two major groups in the Muslim world. They are the Sunnites, who claim to follow the true traditions of Muhammad, and the Shi'ites who are a minority. The most important doctrine of the Shi'ites is belief in the Imams, a doctrine which is rejected by the Sunnites. Since most of the Muslims in Iran, and many in Iraq, Afghanistan, Pakistan, and other lands are Shi'ites, it is necessary to explain their belief. The basic cause for this division among the people of Islam was a difference of opinion as to who should succeed Muhammad. For Muhammad was both a religious and also a civil ruler over most of the people of Arabia. On his death who should continue his rule? The majority of Muslims held that the successor should be the best man in the community, and they accepted the four caliphs who in turn ruled the Muslim empire after Muhammad.

However, from very early times there has been an active minority of Muslims who maintained that ordinary men like Abu Bakr and Umar were not worthy to be the successors of the Prophet of God. They held that only a member of his family should succeed him. And since he had no son who survived him, it was thought that the only rightful successor was Ali, the husband of Fatima, the daughter of Muhammad. Moreover, there was a Shi'ite tradition to the effect that Muhammad formally appointed Ali as his successor. It was believed that Ali appointed his son Hasan to succeed him, and so the succession went by special appointment from one to another in the family of Ali. These men were called "imams" (leaders), and the Muslims who rejected the first three caliphs and accepted the imams were known as "Shi'ites," meaning "partisans" (of Ali). It was their belief that these descendants of Muhammad were truly one with him in spiritual rank, and that the "Light of Muhammad" passed down from one imam to the next, all of whom were thought to be semi-divine beings, sinless, with power to perform very wonderful miracles. They differed from Muhammad only in that they did not bring a new book to replace the Koran, but were part of the Koranic Dispensation.

The Imams and their followers held that they were the rightful political and spiritual rulers of Islam, but the only imam who achieved political rule was Ali, who became the fourth caliph. Some Shi'ites believe in twelve imams, and this sect is the official religion of Iran. Others say the number was seven. Those who hold to twelve say that all except the last were put to death by their enemies, the Sunnites, and they are therefore greatly revered as martyrs. The tombs of some of them in Iraq and Iran are visited annually by hundreds of thousands of pilgrims, many of whom consider a visit to Meshed or Karbala more meritorious than the pilgrimage to Mecca. It is believed that the twelfth imam, who is called the "Mahdi" and the "Lord of the Age," did not die, but disappeared when a child in 873. He will one day return to earth to establish his righteous rule. Some have said that Jesus Christ will come with him to lead his armies in the conquest of the world for the Shi'ite faith.

Belief in the Resurrection and Judgment

One of the chief themes in the early preaching of Muhammad was the resurrection of the dead. At a time known only to God a horrible natural calamity will occur when the earth will be shaken. Then the trumpet will be sounded by the angel Israfil, and all in heaven and on earth will die. Then the trumpet will sound again, all the dead will rise to life, and men and jinn will be called to account. Each one's deeds will be weighed in God's balance, and the record of each will be placed in his hand, in the right hands of the blessed and in the left hands of the damned. Also the bridge Sirat must be crossed, which is very narrow and very long. True believers will be able to cross easily, but the wicked will fall into hell.

Believers, both men and women, who have feared God and been humble and charitable, and have suffered for God's sake, will be welcomed to paradise. There they will dwell forever by flowing rivers, reclining on silken couches, praising God, and enjoying heavenly food and drink in company with dark-eyed maidens. But the unbelieving and the worshipers of other gods will abide in the fires of hell forever, fed with boiling water. Some Muslims interpret these descriptions spiritually, but probably the majority take them literally. It seems that only the martyrs slain in battle for Islam are granted immediate entrance into paradise. All other believers must await the day of resurrection. Between death and the resurrection they are in a very deep sleep. One does not know till that day whether he is to go to hell or to paradise.

RELIGIOUS DUTIES OF MUSLIMS

Since God is the Master, and man is his slave, God has appointed certain tasks which believing men and women must perform. They should perform these tasks not only because God requires it, and in order to escape punishment for failure to do so, but also out of gratitude to God for his goodness. And the doing of these deeds is very meritorious. In the day of judgment they will be weighed in God's balance and will help to cancel the evil deeds which are placed in the other pan of the balance. These sacred duties are sometimes called the "Pillars of Faith," and are usually held to be five: prayers, fasting, alms-giving, pilgrimage to Mecca, and holy war. They are all described by the Arabic word *ibadat* (worship), derived from *abd* (meaning "slave"). These acts are the services a slave renders to his Owner. We will now consider them.

The Prayers (Salat or Namaz)

Wherever one goes throughout the Muslim world he may see men saying the prayers. Every adult believer, male and female, is duty-bound to perform the ritual of worship five times (or among the Shi'ites three times) every day. At the stated times of worship—at daybreak, at noon, in the afternoon, in the evening after sun-set, and in the early part of the night—the call to prayer is sounded forth from minarets and house-tops in tens of thousands of towns and villages, and religious people turn from their ordinary tasks and pray. Some go to the mosques, but most of them say the prayers wherever they are—in the field, by the roadside, in the office or the shop, on the housetop, or in the home.

The worshiper first makes the required ablution with water, then takes his stand facing the Ka'aba in Mecca and recites the appointed phrases in the

Arabic language. He first says "Allahu Akbar" (God is Most Great), then he recites the Fatiheh from the Koran and other Koranic verses. He bows, kneels, and touches his forehead to the ground twice. This completes one *rak'ah* (bowing). During the five times of worship during the day seventeen *rak'ahs* must be performed. The worship is acceptable to God if performed properly, even if the worshiper does not understand the Arabic words he is repeating. No doubt this worship is to some Muslims a spiritual exercise, but for many it is a mechanical act with no moral or spiritual value. The Koran enjoins congregational worship at noon on Friday in the mosque. Women usually recite the prayers in a separate section of the mosque, or at home. In many parts of the Muslim world today those who observe the prayers faithfully are few in number.

Though not required, the believer at the close of the formal worship may say a prayer of his own in his native language. Also on many other occasions such as births, marriages, funerals, etc., prayers are recited in Arabic or the native tongue. And in times of need many ejaculatory prayers are uttered by pious people. Some of the Muslim prayers reveal a true heart-hunger for God. But Muslims do not usually experience the close fellowship with God in prayer which Christians have with their heavenly Father through Christ.

Fasting (Saum or Ruzeh)

Muhammad commanded that the ninth month of the year, which is called Ramadan, be observed as a time of fasting. Since the Muslim calendar is not solar but lunar, a month has about 28 or 29 days, and Ramadan comes each year about ten days earlier than on the previous year. It therefore comes sometimes in winter, when the days are short, and also in summer when the days are long and in some countries very hot. The fast begins when the new moon is seen, and lasts till the next new moon. From the first light of dawn in the morning till about a half hour after sunset in the evening all adults (except the sick and travellers) are forbidden to take food or drink, to smoke, and to have sexual intercourse. Some very strict Muslims will not even swallow their own saliva. If the fast is broken by letting a drop of water go down one's throat while he is cleaning his teeth he must atone by keeping another fast.

For the rich, who can rest in their homes and sleep through the day, Ramadan is not difficult. But for working people the day without food or drink is long and exhausting, as they wait for the signal to let them know they can break the fast. All night they are free to eat, and night is turned to day. It is said there is more feasting in this month than in any other time of the year. There is also much sickness because of the irregularity of the life of the people, and much quarreling because of short tempers. But it is also a time of religious fervor, when special meetings are held in the mosques, and believers try to show their loyalty to their faith by observing its precepts. Ramadan is the most difficult time of year for converts from Islam, for usually great pressure is put on them by family and neighbors to deny their faith in Christ, either by word or by observing this Muslim rite. In modern life it is by no means easy to observe the strict regulations of the fast, and there are many Muslims who do not attempt to do so.

Almsgiving (Zakat)

Since Muhammad was himself once an orphan and poor, it is natural that there should be an emphasis in the Koran on the duty of helping the poor and the orphans. There is what is called the "Purification Tax" for every Muslim, by the payment of which his remaining property becomes lawful to him. It is sometimes stated that this tax for charity should be one-tenth of one's income. In addition, voluntary gifts to charity are encouraged. It sometimes happens that rich people give mosques or schools or hospitals or drinking fountains in discharge of their duty. Probably most people make their gifts to the beggars, who in the past were often found in large numbers in the streets, and who perform an important service by receiving the alms of believers. Beggars do not express appreciation for what they receive, lest they by doing so deprive the giver of the reward which God will give him. It seems that usually the motive for giving is not so much that of showing love to others in need as it is to gain merit for the giver.

The Pilgrimage to Mecca (Hajj)

Muhammad captured Mecca, his birthplace,

which from ancient times had been a sacred city for the Arabs, and made it the center of the religion of Islam. He himself made the Pilgrimage to Mecca and performed all the customary rites, and his example became law for his followers. Every Muslim man and woman who has the means to make the journey to Mecca should do so at least once in his or her life. Accordingly, every year in the month of the Pilgrimage hundreds of thousands of pilgrims from Algeria and Afghanistan, from Java and Syria, from Pakistan and the Sudan, and also from Europe and America and all parts of Africa and other countries, make their way to Mecca. They now travel by plane, ship, train, bus, and camel, enduring the heat which in summer is terrific, and all the hardships and perils of the journey, in order to gain the title of "Hajji," and win the heavenly reward which God will give to everyone who visits the sacred places. Many pilgrims have died on the journey. Those who return to their homes often receive a tremendous welcome from their countrymen, who meet the bus or plane and kiss and embrace the pilgrims, that they too may have a little share in the merit of the Pilgrimage. Unfortunately the journey to Mecca usually produces no moral or spiritual results in the lives of the pilgrims.

The pilgrims assemble at the beginning of the twelfth month of the Muslim year. They make themselves ritually clean, put off their ordinary clothing, and wear only two pieces of cloth wrapped about their bodies. Men may not cover their heads, but women do so. The important acts of the Pilgrimage are the following: going about the Ka'aba[1] seven times; kissing the Black Stone in the wall of the Ka'aba; running between two small hills, Safa and Marwa; drinking from the well Zemzem; halting at various places; visiting the hill Arafat twelve miles east of Mecca; throwing pebbles at three pillars which represent the devil; offering animal sacrifices on the tenth day of the month, in memory of Abraham's sacrifice of his son (who they say is Ishmael), a rite which is observed throughout the Muslim world at the very time that the pilgrims are observing it at Mecca. After this the pilgrims often go to Madina to visit the tomb of Muhammad, and then return to their homes. For millions of Muslims the Pilgrimage has been the outstanding experience of a lifetime. It is a powerful bond of union, holding together peoples of many countries and colors and conditions and tongues and sects, beggars and kings all dressed alike, all united in their faith in Allah and his Apostle, and by their devotion to his Holy House. However, it sometimes happens that individuals have been so deeply disgusted by what they experienced at the Pilgrimage that they gave up their faith in Islam, and a few have become Christians.

Holy War (Jihad)

We learn from the Koran (Sura 9:5) that a revelation came to Muhammad that he should make war on the idolaters of Arabia and force them

[1] The Ka'aba is a simple building, 39 by 33 feet, and 49 feet high.

to submit and become Muslims, and this he did. The followers of Muhammad used the sword to extend their empire throughout the Middle East and North Africa and Spain, and in more recent times pagan peoples have been forcibly brought into the fold of Islam. Some Muslims have always looked forward to a time when they would be able to conquer all non-Muslims and establish Islam as the religio-political system for the world. They see the world divided into two hostile camps, that of the Believers and that of the Infidels, and there must be war till God's army prevails. However, many Muslims today interpret *jihad* (struggle) in a spiritual manner, and say it means a striving for the cause of God. Islam, they maintain, must be advanced not by the sword but by peaceful means, such as missionary effort. Such effort is being actively promoted in many lands, and large numbers of converts are being made to the religion of Islam in some countries.

Other Muslim Practices

In addition to the obligatory duties listed above, there are other practices which are generally observed by Muslims everywhere. One of these is circumcision. Though not commanded in the Koran, it is the custom to circumcise all males in infancy or childhood. Another practice to which great importance has been attached in the past is the veiling of women. Muhammad forbade his wives to appear unveiled, and his example became law for most of the Muslim world. At present the type of veil differs in different places, sometimes covering the woman completely from head to foot, sometimes consisting of only a thin covering on the head. Efforts to abolish the veil have been made in various countries by those concerned about the rights of women, and today in most of the larger cities many or most of the women appear in the streets unveiled. However, in some of the conservative Muslim lands the use of the veil is strictly enforced.

Another generally observed practice is that of abstaining from the eating of food forbidden by the religious law. The Muslim law follows closely the Mosaic law, which forbids the eating of swine's flesh and certain other kinds of meat. Camel flesh is not forbidden by Muslim law as it is in the Old Testament, but the use of alcoholic drinks is forbidden.

It is widely known that polygamy is permitted in Islam. Muhammad set an example in taking at least twelve wives and two concubines, but the Koran limits the number for other believers to four (Sura 4:31). However, they are permitted to marry more than one wife on the condition that they are able to act equitably toward them all. Muslims who today wish to bring the Islamic practices into harmony with modern usages are maintaining that the Koran really commands monogamy, because no man is able to treat "equitably" more than one wife. Also, the increasing cost of living has made it difficult for most men to support more than one household. Whatever the cause may be, it seems that there is much less polygamy than there once was. In some Muslim countries polygamy has been made unlawful, except in unusual circumstances. According to Muslim law, the right of divorce belongs to the man alone, and he is able to divorce his wife at any time for any cause whatever or for no cause. In this matter also women have made courageous efforts in some countries to get justice for themselves, and laws have been made which protect the rights of women. In these and many other ways Christianity has influenced the attitudes of many Muslims.

The reader will have noticed that the duties and practices incumbent on a Muslim are largely external. It would be quite possible for a person of evil character to say the prayers faithfully every day, keep the fast, go to Mecca, eat no pork, and do all that the law requires. It was Jesus, not Muhammad, who said, "Except a man be born again he cannot see the kingdom of God." Only the pure in heart will see God.

4

Differences Between Islam and Christianity

DIFFERENCES BETWEEN ISLAM AND CHRISTIANITY

A Muslim in Teheran or in Toronto says to his Christian friend, "Really, there is no great difference between my religion and yours. We both believe in God, we believe that Jesus was sent by God and was a great prophet, we believe in doing good deeds, and we both hope to be forgiven by God, and to go to paradise when we die. Why should we let our religions divide us? We should stand together in opposition to the people in the world who do not believe in God!" It is indeed true that a Christian has far more in common with a Muslim than he has with a Hindu or Buddhist. In fact there have been those who maintained that Islam is a Christian heresy.

However, as Christians and Muslims discuss their beliefs together, it soon becomes evident that the doctrines which divide them are no fewer than the truths which seem to unite them. If "honesty is the best policy" in business, it is essential in matters of religion. It is therefore unfair to our Muslim friends, as well as disloyal to our faith, to conceal our differences and overlook our misunderstandings for the sake of good relations.

The best relations can be established only on the foundation of understanding and truth. To that end we will now consider some of the important matters in which Muslims and Christians radically disagree.

The Authority of the Bible

There is a basic difference between Christians and Muslims in their attitudes toward the Bible. The historic Christian belief is that the Bible as we now have it is God's Word and is trustworthy. The Koran states that God gave books to some of the prophets, and Muslims accept these books as being from God. They believe in the books of Moses and David and Jesus and other prophets. When a copy of the Bible in his own language is put in his hands, the Muslim may reverently kiss it, and say, "This is the Word of God which the Koran attests." But when he reads it he becomes puzzled. This is not the sort of book which he expected to see. The Koran is all the Word of God, it is God who speaks every verse of it to Muhammad through the angel Gabriel. But in the Bible most of the speakers and writers are men, not God. "This book," he says, "is not like the Koran; it resembles our traditions. This New Testament is not the book which God gave to Jesus, it is written by Matthew and John and Paul. Moreover, there are many things in this book which are contrary to the Koran. It is written here that Noah and David and other holy propets were guilty of gross sin, and this is false. Also it is stated that Jesus was the Son of

God, and died on the cross, contrary to the clear statements of the Koran. So this book is a forgery, and I do not accept it. It is not the original Scripture attested by the Koran."

It is clear from the Koran that Muhammad believed that the Scriptures that were then in the hands of Jews and Christians were authentic, and in no place in the Koran is it suggested that they had been corrupted (Sura 4:48; 10:94). However, when the Jews told Muhammad that he had not been foretold in their books, he charged them with misreading or misinterpreting their Scriptures. Muslims today support their claim that the Bible is untrustworthy by quoting these verses of the Koran. Of course, all the doctrines of Christianity are based on and derived from the Bible. If a Christian has any doubts regarding the authenticity and authority of the Bible, he would do well to resolve these doubts before talking with a Muslim about his faith. If he does not trust the truth of the Bible, he will have no ground to stand on.

The Nature and Character of God

The statement is sometimes made by Christians, "Both the Muslims and Christians believe in one God, and there is surely no justification for our trying to convert them to our religion." However, supposed agreement as to the unity of God does not necessarily imply agreement as to the character of God. Yes, God is One, but what is he like? Is he holy as well as mighty? Is he loving as well as wise? Does he have any concern for sinful men? Has he done something adequate for man's salvation? It is here that the greatest difference between the Christian and Muslim beliefs emerges. According to Islamic doctrine God is all-powerful, and does whatever he wills. He is also merciful and forgiving. But his love is rarely mentioned in the Koran, and there is nothing in Islamic teaching that can compare with the Good News contained in John 3:16, that God has provided a Savior for sinners. All he has done is to send prophets to warn men and to give them books of laws to guide them in the right way. It was pointed out long ago by Raymond Lull, the first great European missionary to Muslims, that the chief lack in the Islamic doctrine of God is the lack of love. The orthodox Muslim could not say, "God is love."

Once a Muslim teacher came to me at night to talk about the Christian religion. I said to him, "Do you agree that love is a very important quality in life?" To this he assented. I then said, "Since this is true, there must certainly be much teaching about love in the books that God has given to men. And if the Koran is, as you believe, the most perfect of God's books, then surely the Koranic teaching about love will be more perfect than that contained in the *Injil* of Jesus, which you say was abrogated by the Koran. Now let me read to you fourteen verses from one chapter of the *Injil* in which the word 'love' is found twenty-seven times, and where we are told that God loves us, and we must love God, and love one

72

another." And I read I John 4:7-21. Then I asked my visitor to read to me what was found in the Koran about God's love and love to men. He was unable to refer to more than a few verses, where it is stated that God loves those who love him, and does not love unbelievers (Sura 3:29). Muslims do not know the wonderful truth that God loves them even though they are sinners, and did all that Almighty God could do to save them from sin and eternal death, by giving his only Son to be the sacrifice for the sin of the world. To the Muslim such an act is considered utterly impossible for God.

Also, the Christian doctrine of the Trinity is both misunderstood and misinterpreted, and rejected by Muslims. "How sad," says a Muslim friend, "that you Christians worship not the one true God but three gods, for you worship Jesus and his mother Mary along with God!" It seems that this is the way in which Muhammad understood the Christian belief in the Trinity (Sura 5:116). And when it is explained that this is not what Christians believe, and the true doctrine of the Trinity is stated, the Muslim still rejects it, saying, "How can three be one?"

Christians often assume that all who believe in one God can agree that God is our heavenly Father. But Muslims cannot call God "Father." Once when I was reading from the sixth chapter of Matthew in Persian to a group of patients waiting to see the doctor in a Christian hospital in Iran, I came to the first words of the Lord's Prayer, "Our Father, which art in heaven." But I was rudely interrupted in my reading. "Don't call God 'father,' " said a man sitting opposite to me, "that is blasphemy, God is not a father!"

On another occasion as I was travelling along the road I saw a farmer threshing his wheat in the field by driving his oxen-drawn sledge round and round over the pile of grain, just as farmers did in the days of Abraham. I turned aside to take his picture, and we were soon engaged in a discussion of religion. Knowing from my dress that I was not a Muslim, the farmer asked, "Who is God?" "God is our Father," I replied. "Not so," said the man emphatically, "for whatever you may think with your mind, God is different from that. God is *not* a father!" If indeed God is thus "different" he is unknowable. Like the people of Athens, many Muslims worship an unknown God.

In Islam God is unknowable because he has not made himself known. The commands of God are made known to men in the Koran, but God himself is not there revealed. And Muhammad never dared to make the claim that he was the revelation of God. Only Jesus Christ, the incarnate Word of God, has been able to say with truth, "He who has seen me has seen the Father. . . . I am in the Father, and the Father [is] in me" (John 14:9-10). As Paul states, "He [Christ] is the image of the invisible God" (Col. 1:15). When one sees Christ he sees God, for "God was in Christ reconciling the world to himself" (II Cor. 5:19). The godly Mahmud Jalily, once a devout Muslim, used to say, "When I was a Muslim I thought I knew God, but I did not. I came to know him truly only when I saw him in Jesus Christ."[1]

A question often asked by Christians is, "Do Muslims have a true knowledge of God? Is Allah the same God whom we worship?" Various answers have been given to these questions. Some have insisted that Allah is a false god, and is quite different from the God and Father of Jesus Christ. Others maintain that Allah is the one true God, the Creator of all things. When Muslims worship their Creator they are surely worshiping the true God. But while they know much about God that is correct, there is much that they do not know, and there are also many of their conceptions which are incorrect. It is as though a person in the dim light of dawn should look at a distant building. He sees the building, he perceives there is only one building, but he is unable to tell whether it is a residence or a factory He is sure it has only one story, and is built of brick. But when he comes nearer, and views the building in the clear light of day, he realizes that it is built of stone, not of brick, and instead of having only one story it has three. He now knows the building as it really is. Just so when a Muslim looks toward God in the imperfect light of Koranic revelation and of his own reason, he sees God's power and will, but he does not see God's love. He sees God's unity, but he does not see that he is Trinity in unity. Such true knowledge

---

[1] William M. Miller, *Ten Muslims Meet Christ* (Grand Rapids: Eerdmans, 1969), pp. 133-147.

of God is possible only when one sees God in his Son Jesus Christ.

The Relationship of Jesus Christ to God

Christians believe in the Trinity in unity because they, like the early disciples, believe that Jesus Christ is the only Son of God and one with his Father. But when the Christian speaks of Jesus as "Son of God," the Muslim may reply with horror, "You really don't think that God took a wife and had a son, do you?" Thinking of sonship in only the physical sense, the Muslim misunderstands and is repelled by the title which Christians delight to give to their Lord (Sura 2:110). Even when it is explained that Christ's sonship is spiritual and not physical, and that he was from eternity the Son of God, the Muslim remains unhappy and unconvinced. Of course if Jesus is not God's Son, then it follows that God is not a Father. It should be noted that only those who believe that Jesus is indeed the Son of God can rightly address God as "Father."

Muslims believe that Jesus was born of the Virgin Mary, but they explain that this does not make him "Son of God." For he was created by God in the womb of Mary without a human father, as Adam was created by God of dust without either father or mother. Muslims highly honor Jesus for his remarkable miracles, knowing that he healed the sick, and even raised the dead to life. If one wishes to compliment a physician in Iran he may say, "Doctor, you perform miracles; you have the breath of Jesus!" Many Muslims have a sincere affection for Jesus Christ as a kind and loving prophet.

But they do not know the vastness of his love, for they refuse to believe that he loved sinners so much that he voluntarily died on the cross to save them. In wishing to honor Jesus they say that he was so great it was impossible for his enemies to overcome and kill him. Moreover, God is just, and he would never have permitted his holy and righteous prophet Jesus to suffer the shame of the cross. It is generally believed that God performed a miracle to save Jesus. He changed one of the enemies to look like Jesus, and he was taken and crucified by mistake in the place of Jesus, whom God took alive to heaven, where he is today.

If Jesus Christ is not truly one with God, and if he did not die, there is no adequate sacrifice for the sin of the world, and sinners have no Savior. We are still in our sins. Also, there is no glorious resurrection on the third day, no joyous Easter, and no victory over death and sin. Thus Muslims have no assurance of forgiveness, or of eternal life with God. For them death has not lost its sting, or grave its victory. How desperately they need to know and believe the message of the cross and the empty tomb! It is believed that Jesus will one day return from heaven, will punish pagans, Jews, and Christians for their failure to accept Muhammad, God's last and greatest Prophet, and will help establish Islam as the one true religion of the world. How very different is the Muslim conception of Jesus Christ from that revealed by God in the Bible!

The Absence of a Prediction of Muhammad in the Bible

The Muslim is sure that as Moses and other prophets foretold the coming of Jesus, so Jesus must have foretold the coming of Muhammad. In fact the Koran states that Jesus did predict the coming of "Ahmad," whom they say was Muhammad. Since no such prediction is found in the New Testament, Muslims conclude that it was removed from the *Injil* by Christians at the time of Muhammad's appearance, because they did not want to believe on him. One charge which is frequently heard is that Jesus in John 16:7 referred to Muhammad when he said he would go away and send the Paraclete (Comforter). Some Muslim scholars have asserted that Jesus in this prediction used the Greek word *periclutos,* which means "praised." In Arabic the word "muhammad" means the "praised one." So Jesus, they say, promised that Muhammad would come. But Christians changed the word to *paracletos* (comforter), to excuse themselves for rejecting Muhammad.

Once when I was in Rome I obtained permission to look at this verse in the original Greek text of the ancient manuscript, the Codex Vaticanus, which was written long before the time of Muhammad. After that I was able to assure those who brought this false charge against the Christians that I had seen and examined carefully the original text of this manuscript, and was convinced that it had not been changed. Jesus promised the Comforter, not Muhammad. However, even such assurances do not satisfy those whose purpose it is to reject Christian truths.

Jesus is indeed honored by Muslims, but they believe that a more honorable one than he has come, and Jesus must yield the highest seat to him. This was symbolized in a large poster which I once saw in Iran. Formerly artists were not permitted to paint pictures of Muhammad's face. But pictures of Christ and other prophets became quite popular and were bought and treasured by Muslims. So the artists of Iran began to make money by producing paintings of the Prophet of Arabia, with the Koran in his hand. In the poster to which I refer, a whole series of small pictures copied from American Sunday School cards, representing Moses and Joshua and David and John the Baptist and Jesus and others, were arranged in a circle. Then in the center of the circle was a large head of Muhammad, the greatest of the prophets. The central place, which belonged to Jesus Christ, had been given to another! Jesus had become just one of the prophets.

Thus between the Jesus of Muslim belief and the Christ of the Bible there is a great gulf fixed. "Who say ye that I am?" asks Jesus. "You are one of the Great Prophets," reply the Muslims. "No, you are the Son of the living God!" say Peter and all those to whom the truth has been revealed by God.

The Nature of Man

Another radical difference between Islamic and Christian beliefs is seen in the conception of man's nature and needs. Christians and Muslims agree that Adam disobeyed God and was punished by being expelled from the Garden. According to Muslim doctrine, no change took place in Adam's nature as a result of this act. He was able to obey God perfectly after his disobedience as he was before, and his descendants suffered no ill effect from their first parents' error. They were able to obey God fully if they knew what was required of them, and if they had sufficient encouragement. They were not by nature sinful, but weak and ignorant. And so they were in need not of a Savior but of teachers and guides, who would give them God's commandments and warn them of the terrible consequences of disobedience. So God in mercy sent prophets to instruct and warn them, and guide them in the right way.

The Christian conception, on the other hand, is that man was created in God's image to be not a slave but a son to God. But Adam by his act of disobedience "fell," and was radically changed. He became a slave of sin, and his descendants inherited his sinful nature. Adam and his descendants were unable to do what God required, and their need was not so much for instruction as for new hearts. They had become enemies of God and needed to be reconciled. They needed the Lamb of God, who would die for them and make expiation for their sins. They needed a divine Savior. To meet that need the Son of God came to earth and died and rose again. Those slaves of sin who believe in him are born again and become children of God.

I once had a friend whose name was Abdullah, which means "slave of God." I said to him, "If you believe in Jesus Christ you will become a child of God. Isn't it better to be a son than a slave?" He smiled and replied, "For me it is enough to be God's slave!" I longed for him to become a member of our Father's family, but he would not.

The Way of Salvation

Another important difference between Islam and Christianity is in the answer to the question, "What must I do to be saved?" The Christian answers, as did Paul in the prison in Philippi, "Believe in the Lord Jesus, and you will be saved" (Acts 16:31). Salvation is God's free gift to those who put their trust in Christ, and cannot be earned by one's good deeds. "For by grace you have been saved through faith; and this is not your own doing, it is the gift of God" (Eph. 2:8). The answer of the Muslim is, "Believe in God and in his Apostle Muhammad, and do what God requires, and if God so wills he will accept you." The sinner is pointed not to Christ, who died to take away the sin of the world, but to another. And we recall the words of Paul to the Galatians, "If anyone is preaching to you a gospel contrary to that which you received, let him be accursed" (Gal. 1:9). This is indeed a different "gospel."

Islam has no Savior. Muhammad is rarely called Savior. He is said to have brought God's laws to men, and they by keeping those laws must satisfy God's requirements and win his approval. We have in a previous chapter described the duties which God the Master has commanded men who are his slaves to perform. The Koran refers to the "balance" in which God on the day of judgment will weigh the deeds of every individual. The good deeds will be placed in one pan of the balance, and the evil deeds in the other. If the good deeds are heavier the believer will go to the paradise described in the Koran as a place of sensual enjoyment. If one's evil deeds are heavier, he will be cast into the fires of hell. It would seem that one would need to be only fifty-one percent good to get into paradise. This is quite different from what is said about entrance into God's holy city. We are told that "nothing unclean shall enter it, nor anyone who practices abomination or falsehood, but only those who are written in the Lamb's book of life" (Rev. 21:27).

Since many Muslims realize that they are not even half good, they recite extra prayers in addition to those required for each day, they make gifts to charity, and go on pilgrimages not only to Mecca but also to other sacred shrines, in order to gain merit and if possible balance their account with God. But since God does not make known how the accounts of his servants stand, a Muslim facing death does not know whether he is to go to paradise or to hell. After all, the decision is made by the arbitrary will of God, and no one can predict what that decision will be.

Once in the days before auto transport I was travelling by donkey from the sacred city of Meshed in northeast Iran to the town of Nishapur, where is the tomb of the famous poet Omar Khayyam. As I walked beside the donkey I caught up with a group of men and women who also were travelling by donkey and on foot. They were pilgrims who had come to Meshed from a place hundreds of miles away, and were returning to their homes. I greeted them, and walked and talked with them as we journeyed.

"Did you often visit the tomb of the Imam Reza while you were in Meshed?" I asked.

"Oh yes," one man replied, "we visited the sacred tomb two times each day while we were in Meshed. We prayed and shed tears over the grave of the martyr, as we remembered his sufferings, and we asked God to forgive us."

"Now you are going home," I continued, "are you sure that God has accepted your pilgrimage and forgiven your sins?"

"Oh no," said the man, "only God knows that."

And so the Muslim lives and dies, not sure of his final salvation. He can only hope for the mercy of God, hope that the angels or the Prophet will intercede for him in the last day, and he will be saved from hell. How the Christian longs for his Muslim friends to have the same assurance that he has, based not on his hopes but on the promises of God, that his sins have been forgiven because of Christ's death, and he now has eternal life because of Christ's resurrection, and nothing can separate him from God's love in Christ!

Some Other Differences

There are many other differences between the two religions. One that is important to converts from Islam in non-Arabic-speaking lands is that in Christian worship the believer may speak to God in his mother tongue, whereas in Islam he is compelled to pray in Arabic, which he does not fully understand. Also in Islam the harmony of the home is often destroyed by the quarreling of several wives. A young man once said to me, "My home is hell, for my father has four wives and they are always fighting." Sad to say, there is not always love and harmony in homes where God's law of monogamy is observed. But the love and peace of a truly Christian home are seldom found in homes where polygamy is practiced.

Finally, it should be realized that Islam has sought to bring men back under the dispensation of law, from which Christ delivered believers. "Christ redeemed us from the curse of the law," wrote Paul to the Galatians. Whether it be God's law revealed in the Bible, or the less perfect law given in the Koran, no one can hope by keeping the law to be accepted by God, for no one (except Christ) has ever kept perfectly either the Mosaic or the Islamic law. And so, "All who rely on the works of the law are under a curse; for it is written, 'Cursed be every one who does not abide by all things written in the book of the law. and do them' " (Gal. 3:10, 13). Christ delivered those who put their trust in him from the bondage and the curse of the law by dying in their place. He made them children of God and gave them his Holy Spirit to make them holy. Then Islam, coming six hundred years after Christ, brought those who submitted to it back into bondage, for it is a legalistic system. Those who had become God's sons and daughters are invited, or compelled in some instances, to become God's slaves. Those whose sins had been freely forgiven for Christ's sake are required to earn God's favor and forgiveness by works of merit—prayers and fasts and pilgrimages and animal sacrifices. It is the privilege and duty of all who love Christ to tell the Good News of freedom to these slaves of law, and to say to those who believe: "For freedom Christ has set us free; stand fast therefore, and do not submit again to a yoke of slavery" (Gal. 5:1).

Islam and Christianity are two roads. At first glance they seem to be similar, both leading in the same direction. But on closer examination it becomes evident that between them as they advance a great rift appears, and they take the traveller in two different directions. One leads to life, and the other to death. For only Christ is the Way to life eternal and to God the Father.

5
Mountains to Be Moved

MOUNTAINS TO BE MOVED

During the past century the expansion of the Christian movement has been greater than in any century since the first. As the result of labors of missionaries from abroad and devoted Christians in all parts of the world, untold millions of our fellowmen have heard the Good News of Christ and have been gathered into his church. The Christians of Korea believe that in a few more decades their country will be predominantly Christian. It is predicted that in the near future the majority of people in Africa will profess the Christian faith. In other lands which a century ago were largely pagan there are now strong and growing Christian communities. It is quite evident that Christ is with his followers as he promised to be, and that the gospel is still the power of God to salvation for all who believe, be they from east or west, north or south.

But there is at least one portion of the population of the earth in which the response to the gospel has been different. In what is called the "Muslim world," that is, the eight hundred or more millions of people who constitute about one-sixth of the world's population and who profess the faith of Islam, the number of conversions to

Christianity has been small indeed, with the one outstanding exception of Indonesia. A text on which Dr. Samuel Zwemer used often to preach when he was in America was: "Master, we toiled all night and took nothing! But at your word I will let down the nets" (Luke 5:5). "Fishers of men" have truly in some Muslim lands toiled not just "all night" but all through years and decades without having seen souls saved or churches of converts established. In fact, in some of the lands of the Middle East like Syria, Turkey, Egypt, Iraq, and Iran, members of the ancient Christian churches have lived in close and often friendly contact with Muslims for some 1,300 years without having been able to draw any considerable number of them to faith in Christ. On the contrary, it is probable that many millions of Christians have during this period for various reasons professed faith in Islam.

Why So Few Converts to Christianity?

Missionaries to Muslims have continually searched their own souls and have studied and restudied their message and their methods, if they might perhaps find the reasons for their failure to accomplish among the people of Islam what God had enabled their fellow-workers to do in non-Muslim lands. "Is it because we are not filled with the Holy Spirit?" they ask themselves. And they meet together to confess their sins and pray for the power of the Spirit which Christ promised to his disciples (Acts 1:8). "Is it because we have not prayed in faith?" they ask.

Then days of special prayer are arranged, and earnest requests are made of their supporters that they pray for Muslims and for all Christians seeking to save them. "Is it because there are so few Christians who are endeavoring to lead Muslims to Christ?" Then renewed efforts are made by prayer to the "Lord of the harvest," and by appeals to Christians, to secure volunteers for the neglected task of evangelizing Muslims.

"Or," say the missionaries, "perhaps our methods have all been wrong. We have established schools and hospitals, when we should have given priority to evangelism. We have dealt with individuals, when we should have tried to draw whole families or groups into the church. We have unintentionally presented Christianity as a Western religion, and not a product of the East. We have tried to draw people out of their Islamic culture, instead of encouraging them to be 'friends of Jesus' while they remain in Islam and worship in the mosque with their Muslim brothers. And instead of carrying on a controversy with Muslim opponents, we should have dialogue with our Muslim brothers, the purpose of which will be not conversion but mutual understanding."

Also, it is sometimes proposed that our message must be adapted to the conceptions of Muslims. The title Son of God should not be used of Christ, the doctrine of the Trinity should be avoided, and the unity of God be proclaimed. The humanity and prophethood of Jesus rather than his deity should be stressed, and the similarities of Islam and Christianity instead of the differences should be emphasized. The hope has been expressed that in such ways as these the causes of conflict might be avoided, and Muslims might be drawn closer to "Jesus son of Mary," as he is called in the Koran.

No doubt all of these efforts to accomplish more effectively the task of making disciples which was entrusted by Christ to his Church have been of value, as Christians have humbly sought the guidance of God's Word and God's Spirit, and have learned from the experiences of their fellow-workers in non-Muslim lands. However, there has not resulted as yet from these efforts any appreciable increase in the number of conversions of Muslims, or in the success of those who have attempted to establish indigenous churches in Muslim communities.

The Strength of Islam

When an influential Korean Christian was asked why in his opinion Christianity had been able to make such remarkable progress in such a short time in his country, he replied that the people of Korea had no real religion, no faith in anything adequate to sustain them. And when they heard the message of a loving God and a Savior they welcomed and accepted it. If this was true of the Koreans it is most certainly not true of most Muslims. Certainly one reason why they have not responded more to the Christian message is that Islam is a highly developed religion, with a Book supposed to be the Word of God, and a theology, and a long and in some respects a brilliant history. It contains much that is true and good. Its teachings are in some instances easier to understand and believe than are the mysteries of the Trinity and the divine-and-human nature of Christ. The duties required by Islam, though by no means easy, are in the range of man's ability to perform. Once an educated Muslim said to me, "Islam is better for the world than Christianity." When I asked his reason he replied, "It is possible for one to obey the teachings and laws of Islam, but the teachings of Christ are so lofty that no one is able to obey them."

Moreover, since in this age of progress it is generally thought that the latest is the best, surely, it is said, Islam must be better than Christianity which preceded it by six hundred years! This is of course the claim made in the Koran, that Islam is God's final and most perfect revelation. For these and other reasons Muslims are convinced that their religion is the best, and meets their needs, and should not be abandoned for any other.

Christian Doctrines Contrary to the Koran

It is assumed that the Koran is God's Word, and therefore infallible, and any teaching which is contrary to the Koran is most certainly false. Hence when the Christian tells the Muslim that Jesus is indeed the Son of God and one with God, that he truly died on the cross, was buried, and rose again, that he did not foretell the coming of Muhammad but warned his followers against false prophets, and that it is he who will raise the dead to life and sit as Judge of all men, the Muslim is forced either to reject all this Christian doctrine which is contrary to the Koran, or to reject the Koran and Muhammad and the whole system of Islam and put his trust in Christ alone. Knowing how very difficult it is to reject convictions one has had from childhood, it is not surprising that Muslims almost always choose the former alternative.

When Christian evangelists at home or abroad meet with great success they say, "See what God has done!" They believe that their success is proof that God was with them. In just the same way the Muslim points to the amazing success of Muhammad, who alone at first and then with a few followers, was able to make himself master of all Arabia. And within a hundred years after his death the Muslim empire extended from Spain in the West to central Asia in the East. "Is not this proof of God's approval of Islam?" asks the Muslim. "If God had not given his blessing, could it have won the allegiance of one-sixth of the population of the world?" What believer in Almighty God can say that this tremendous success of Islam and its influence on the world happened without God's permission?

Islam a Religio-Political System

It must be remembered that Islam is not only a personal religious faith but is also a religio-political system in which "church and state," so to speak, are united. The laws of Islam are both civil and religious, and no distinction is made. Thus Islam includes all aspects of life—personal, social, economic, cultural, religious, and political.

The law of their faith tells the Muslim man and woman what their duties are in all areas of their life on earth.

The Muslim belongs to a community, in which he functions as a member. From birth to death he lives a life which is related to other members of the community. Detaching one from the community is like cutting off a member of the body. How can it live if severed from the other members? To cut oneself off from the Islamic community in order to become a Christian seems to a Muslim like committing suicide. Even if he is willing to do this for his own salvation, is it right for him to break the heart of his parents, to lose his Muslim wife, who cannot legally live with a non-Muslim, and so wreck his home? And the problems which a woman faces are even greater than those facing a man.

According to Islamic law, the penalty for apostasy is death. In some countries a Muslim who is baptized, or who has only shown interest in Christianity, may quite possibly be poisoned by his own family. In countries in which Islam is the national religion the abandonment of Islam is considered an act of disloyalty to the state. The convert to Christianity is suspected of being in the employ of some foreign government as a spy. "Only within the last two months," writes a reporter from a Muslim land, "one who was rather free in the use of cross-cultural media, was threatened by legal authorities, who stated that if anyone should accept Christianity both he and the one converting [him] would be killed. The threat of severest legal action was made against another because it had come to the attention of the Society of Islamic Affairs that tracts and booklets were being distributed for the purpose of propagating the Christian religion." In places where there is greater tolerance the convert to Christianity may not be in danger of losing his life, but he may lose his job, and his friends, and his family. The convert is rare who does not have a heavy cross to carry as he follows Christ. There are probably many seekers for God throughout the Muslim world who desire to become Christians, but who find it impossible to pay the price.

Failure of Churches to Welcome Converts

Another reason why some Muslims do not become Christians is that they are not attracted to or welcomed by the churches with which they are acquainted. In some countries there are Oriental churches which trace their history back to apostolic times, the members of which for various cultural and political reasons do not feel friendly toward Muslims, and do not want Muslim converts to attend their church services. Sometimes the conduct of some Christians is unworthy of Christ, and Muslims get the impression that Christians are a quarrelsome people, or that the marks of being a Christian are eating pork and drinking wine. Even in countries like Pakistan and India, where there are rather large Catholic and Protestant churches of more recent origin, the members of these churches who are chiefly from a Hindu background are frequently unwilling to welcome

Muslim converts into their fellowship. So the convert, expelled from the Islamic community, does not find another community in which he feels at home. Till now it has not often happened that there have been enough converts in one place to constitute a strong group or church of those who have come out of Islam.

Loss of Converts

Because of lack of fellowship and support from a strong and loving Christian community, and for various other reasons, the proportion of converts who in some countries have fallen away is large. The pastor rejoices that a Muslim has broken with Islam, has professed faith in Christ, has had months of teaching and testing, and has finally been baptized and received into a Christian group or church. The new believer becomes a faithful and fearless Christian witness, and leads others to faith in Christ. Then after a time he becomes careless about church attendance, loses his "first love," removes himself from the Christian group, and finally becomes one of the "lost sheep." He may return to Islam, but usually gives up all concern about religion. Every effort is made to bring him back, but to no avail.

What happened to this beloved brother (or sister)? Was he never a true believer? How often some member of a "Christian race" has said to a missionary when he saw a convert from Islam fall away, or even disgrace the cause of Christ by some evil deed, "You are very naive to imagine that a Muslim can become a Christian! It is impossible for a Muslim to change his religion, and you are wasting your time preaching to Muslims." Yet it seemed that this new believer had all the marks of being a true Christian! Were the world, the flesh and the devil too strong for him to oppose? Did his Christian friends fail him? Why did not the Good Shepherd keep him, as he promised to keep his sheep? How we have agonized over these lost members of the flock! After having suffered several heart-breaking experiences of failures like this, the Christian evangelist is tempted by the devil to give up the task as hopeless. If he does so, and ceases to labor and pray in hope for the conversion of others, he may be saved much suffering, but sinners will not be saved.

Decrease of Interest in Religion Among Muslims

Formerly it frequently happened in some countries that individuals or groups would visit the Christian missionary or pastor for the purpose of proving to him the superiority of Islam and the errors of Christianity. These confrontations were not always friendly, but they gave to the Christian an opportunity not only to explain and defend his faith, but also to show patience and love to hostile men. However, these men were deeply interested in religious matters. But in recent times it seems that as a result of the extension of secular education, and the absorption of many of the educated people in making money and acquiring cars, radios, and all the good things of modern life, there is in many parts of the Muslim world a growing decrease in interest in religion.

Such people may not say the prayers or keep the month of fasting or go on pilgrimage to Mecca or visit a Christian to discuss religious matters with him, but they strongly profess that they are Muslims. To them Islam is a precious cultural heritage rather than a personal faith. They consider "religion" a burden which they do not need and do not wish to carry, but they are ready to defend Islam if it should be criticized. Some Christians had hoped that modern education and close contacts with the non-Muslim world would break the bonds of Islam, and prepare liberated Muslims for coming to Christ to find true freedom. But these hopes have not been realized to any extent. For it appears that an irreligious Muslim is usually no more ready to become a Christian than was his devout grandfather. He thinks Christianity is, like Islam, a useless burden, and does not realize it is the one power which will enable him to bear the heavy burdens of life. He does not know that Christ's "burden is light."

Difficulties Created by Political Events

The work of evangelization is very directly affected by events in the political world. When, a half-century ago, most of the Muslim countries were under the control of Western nations, Christian missionaries from the West were in some of these countries permitted to carry on their work with great freedom, but in others they were severely restricted by the Western political authorities in their efforts to preach and win converts. During the past twenty-five years most of the Muslim countries have achieved their independence, and have established either Muslim or secular states. In some the freedom formerly given to Christians to propagate their faith has been continued, but in others it has been greatly diminished. And it has become difficult or impossible for missionaries from some countries to obtain visas to enter certain countries in which Islam is dominant.

For example, as a result of aid given by the United States of America to Israel in the 1967 war with some of the Arab nations, all American missionaries were expelled from certain Arab countries. Sad to say, this brought to an end, at least temporarily, much of the patient and loving effort of many years to make Christ known in those countries by word and by deed. It has also resulted in increased opposition throughout the Muslim world to all efforts to convert Muslims to the Christian faith.

It is often forgotten that in Soviet Russia and in China there are untold millions of Muslims. Before these great empires became communist, a number of courageous missionaries were seeking to make Christ known to the followers of Muhammad in remote regions of Central Asia. Now no missionaries from the West are permitted to enter these "closed lands." But occasionally reports come out that Muslims are being converted by Chinese and Russian Christians. Lands closed to missionaries are not necessarily closed to Christians, and there are many followers of Christ who are quietly witnessing to Muslims by their love and also by their words in places where there is no religious freedom. The only city in the Muslim world which Christians may not enter is Mecca.

The history of Indonesia reveals clearly the way in which political happenings affect evangelism. As a result of Dutch rule for several hundred years, and the policies of the government regarding religion, millions of people in Indonesia, including some Muslims, had become Christians. In 1965, when Communists were about to take control of the government, there was an upsurge of anti-Communist forces, and large numbers of people with Communist sympathies were slaughtered. Then it was decreed that everyone must have a religion. It is said that many people who were not closely attached to any religion, including Muslims, decided to join the Christians, who had taken no part in the massacres. And so the churches received very large numbers of new members, some of whom were former Muslims. It is stated that God's Spirit produced a true conversion in the lives of many of these converts. Yet it was the change in the political situation which brought most of them into the churches.

Paucity of Laborers for the Harvest

When the Lord Jesus saw the multitudes, he said to his disciples, "The harvest is plentiful, but the laborers are few; pray therefore the Lord of the harvest to send laborers into his harvest" (Matt. 9:37-38). If there is to be an ingathering there must be enough laborers to sow the seed and water it and at harvest time gather the sheaves. As Paul wrote, "How are they to believe in him of whom they have not heard? And how are they to hear without a preacher" (Rom. 10:14)? Certainly, in addition to other difficulties which have been mentioned, one important reason for the scarcity of converts in the Muslim world has been the tragic lack of laborers. It seems that for centuries the Christians of the world had little desire to lead Muslims to Christ. Many thousands of zealous but misguided Christians went forth from Europe to fight the Muslims in the Crusades. But how many went with the "sword of the Spirit," which is the Word of God, to tell them of Christ's love and salvation? There were very few.

In recent times God has called a number of laborers, faithful men and women, to devote themselves to the task of taking the gospel to the people of Islam. But because of the hardness of the soil and the lack of results in Muslim communities, most of the efforts of Christians, both Western and Eastern, have been devoted to the evangelization of pagan people who are more ready to accept the gospel. It must be confessed that, with some glorious exceptions, the Christians of the world have signally failed to obey Christ by sending laborers to sow and reap a harvest in Muslim lands.

Even today the proportion of missionaries,

from both the East and the West, working in Muslim areas with the definite purpose of leading Muslims to faith in Christ, compared with those seeking to convert non-Muslims, is pitifully small. "He who sows sparingly will also reap sparingly, and he who sows bountifully will also reap bountifully" (II Cor. 9:6).

Revival of Islam

A few decades ago it appeared that in many parts of the world Islam was a dying religion. But that is not the case today, for it seems that new life has come to Islam. Muslim missionaries are being trained in Egypt and other places, and are being sent out to convert pagan peoples. It is reported that very large sums of money are being given by Muslim countries in the Middle East to establish schools and hospitals in Africa and to convert black Africans to Islam. Political and even military power is sometimes used for this purpose.

As has been explained, Islam is a religio-political system, and may be properly used for political purposes. Muslim nations that are attempting to become strong and independent will therefore encourage religious devotion in order to unite and inspire their people, and will oppose all efforts of those who would create division, whether they be Communists or Christians. Hence, converting Muslims to Christianity may be considered more a political than a religious offense.

Not only in Africa and the East but also in the

West active missionary work is being carried on by Muslims. Mosques have been built and Islamic centers have been established in various cities, both for the purpose of holding the allegiance of the large Muslim groups now resident in Europe and America, and also to win converts from the native populations. Many black people have become "Black Muslims," and some, both black and white, have become orthodox Muslims. Islam is indeed at our very door. It has been well said that it is "Christianity's greatest challenge."

The Resistance of the Enemy

Finally, there is one obstacle to the conversion and salvation of Muslims which is everywhere present. This is the opposition to the gospel of the one whom Jesus referred to as "the enemy," "the evil one," and "Satan." He attempted to defeat Jesus himself by quoting the Word of God to him. But Jesus won the victory, bound the "strong man," and set free his captives. The apostles of Jesus also were well aware that men were held captive by Satan, and their warfare was not with flesh and blood but with the "spiritual hosts of wickedness" (Eph. 6:12).

Christ's servants have always known that Satan is still actively opposing the work of God. However, it has seemed to those who have sought to save Muslims that Satan has made a special effort to hold them in his power. Some have expressed the opinion that Islam itself is Satan's most brilliant and effective invention for leading men astray, and that the "revelations" which came to Muhammad were not from God but from the devil. Since Satan is a liar and the father of lies (John 8:44), every teaching which is contrary to the true Word of God has its origin in him, whether it be in a Christian pulpit in America or in a mosque in Arabia. We are told that Satan often comes disguised as "an angel of light" (II Cor. 11:14), and by speaking what is good and true (which is from God, the source of all truth), he attempts to accomplish his own evil purpose.

As the Good News of Christ is proclaimed to Muslims, "the god of this world has blinded the minds of the unbelievers to keep them from seeing the light of the gospel of the glory of Christ, who is the likeness of God" (II Cor. 4:4). When the invitation of Christ is extended, "Come unto me and I will give you rest!," Satan darkens their minds and paralyzes their wills, so that they are unable to understand and to resolve to believe and be saved. How vividly are Christians in Muslim lands aware of the presence and power of the enemy! From a country closed to missionaries this word has come: "In this pioneer work there's not much 'success' to write home about, but of one thing we're certain: we are on Satan's territory. If the fierceness of the battle indicates that ground is being gained, something great must be happening, for the Enemy is hard at work! Pray that we may recognize Satan's tactics and be constantly on the offensive." In this conflict we know that the serpent's head was bruised by Christ on the cross, and his end is sure. So we can sing with Luther:

> And though this world, with devils filled,
> Should threaten to undo us;
> We will not fear, for God hath willed
> His truth to triumph through us:
> The Prince of darkness grim,
> We tremble not for him;
> His rage we can endure,
> For lo! his doom is sure,
> One little word shall fell him.

As Christians we face these mighty mountains of difficulty which seem to block the advance of the gospel in Muslim lands and in Muslim minds and hearts, Christ's word comes to us: "I say to you, if you have faith as a grain of mustard seed, you will say to this mountain, 'Move hence to yonder place,' and it will move; and nothing will be impossible to you." With men the task is indeed impossible, but with God all things are possible. He is the "God of the impossible."

6
From Darkness to Light

FROM DARKNESS TO LIGHT

However great difficulties may be, nothing is too hard for God. The giving of new life to a person dead in sin and unbelief requires a miracle, whether the new birth occurs in America or in Arabia. Almighty God, who has saved millions of sinners in all parts of the world, is abundantly able to perform this same miracle in Muslim lives, and he will do so whenever and wherever he wills.

When I went to Iran in 1919 I shared the faith of the devoted group of missionaries who were in that land that the gospel is the power of God, and that I would see with my own eyes Muslims transformed into children of God through faith in Jesus Christ. At that time there were a few converts from Islam in several of the churches. But in the years that followed God gave us the joy of witnessing a number of his miracles of salvation, and of being blessed by fellowship in Christ with men and women who had become our beloved brothers and sisters through faith in him. The stories of some of these Christians have been related in the book, *Ten Muslims Meet Christ*.[1]

[1] William M. Miller, *Ten Muslims Meet Christ* (Grand Rapids: Eerdmans, 1969).

Also the stories of seven other converts from Islam in other countries are told in *The True Path*.[2] In this chapter I wish to tell of others whom I knew intimately in Iran, that some of the ways in which God has accomplished his loving purpose of salvation may be made known.

The Sardar of Seistan

"I have good news for you!" exclaimed the young bookseller Hopeful as he entered my room. "In Seistan I met a man who is a Christian. He is a man of importance, the head of a tribe on the border of Afghanistan. He openly professes his faith in Christ, and when I was a guest in his home he urged the other chieftains who were there to buy my Christian books. Once when these chieftains were planning to make war on the central government he persuaded them not to do so, saying that he was a Christian and Christ had forbidden warfare. How I wish you could visit Sardar Nazar Khan!" Sardar means "chief."

I was delighted and surprised to hear this report. For when I was a young missionary I spent some months in Seistan, trying to sell Scripture portions to the ignorant and bigoted Muslims in the dirty bazaar, and praying and hoping to find interested inquirers, who never came to me. It had been a time of bitter discouragement, the most difficult I had ever known. And now I am

2 Mark Hanna, *The True Path* (P.O. Box 2581, Colorado Springs, Colo. 80901: International Doorways Publishers, n.d.).

told there is a Christian in Seistan! I wondered how this Muslim had become a believer in Christ. True, there had been an English mission in that region for a few years, but only a faithful Indian doctor and his wife remained. Had the Sardar been converted through them? I hoped some day to go to see him myself.

But Seistan is more than 600 miles south of Meshed, where I was stationed, and travel was difficult. However, at last the time came when I was able to accompany Hopeful on another journey to that region. We travelled in the front seat of a truck bound for Zahedan, the terminus of the Baluchistan railway, which is about seventy miles from Seistan. Hopeful was eager to go to Seistan to find the Sardar, but we lacked both time and transportation. "If only he knew you are here he would surely come to Zahedan to see us," said Hopeful. But there was little hope that he would do so.

We delayed our departure one day in order to give the communion to an English family who had not been able to commune for a very long time, there being no minister in that region. This delay was indeed of God, for Hopeful came back from his book selling in the bazaar with the good news that he had seen the Sardar. "He has just arrived from Seistan," he explained, "and is the guest of the governor. He was thrilled to know that you are here, and will come to see you at three o'clock this afternoon."

Eagerly I awaited the arrival of the Sardar. I pictured to myself what he would look like, wearing the baggy white pantaloons of the Baluchi tribesmen, with a big white turban wrapped around his head, and a thick black beard adorning his face. But when at three o'clock he entered the home of the doctor where I was a guest, great was my surprise to see coming to me a clean-shaven and neatly dressed gentleman who looked like an official from Teheran. He shook my hand warmly, and smiled at me as though he were greeting an old friend, and we sat down to have tea.

"Pardon my curiosity," I said, "but I have heard that you are a Christian. Will you kindly tell me who told you about Christ?"

"Yes," replied my visitor, "I have been a Christian for twenty years. But no one told me about Christ."

"Then how did you become a Christian?" I inquired.

"Through reading the Bible," he replied.

"But where did you get a Bible?" I asked. I thought he had perhaps purchased one when he was in Bombay or Teheran.

The Sardar smiled, and said quietly, "I got it from you."

"Do you mean that when I was in Seistan twenty years ago you saw me and bought a Bible from me?" I asked in amazement.

"Yes," he replied, "I was then a boy about sixteen years of age. I came to your room and asked for a big Persian Bible. You sold a copy to me, and told me it was the Word of God and should be treated with respect. I took it to my home in the village, read it by myself, and believed on Christ. Seven years passed, and then one of those English missionaries who were here baptized me and gave me the communion. I had a celebration in my house to which I invited the other chieftains, and I put a cross on the wall to show them that I was a Christian."

"That is indeed wonderful!" I said. "How long has it been since you took the communion?"

The Sardar replied that he had communed only once, when he was baptized thirteen years ago. So early next morning, just before we left for Meshed, he came to the doctor's home, and we broke the bread and drank from the cup, as we remembered our crucified and living Lord.

Years later the Sardar visited me in Teheran, and attended church there. He still professed his faith in Christ. Then in a severe political disturbance in Seistan both he and the governor were brutally murdered by enemies of the government. Whether his being a Christian was the cause of his death is not known. I believe he died in the faith.

Almost every convert to Christianity in Iran was influenced in his decision by reading the Bible. Even though Muslims have been told that the Christian Scriptures have been corrupted and are now untrustworthy, the Bible is indeed the "sword of the Spirit," and is able to convince openminded readers that it is true.

A Page from the Book

One day a shoemaker in Meshed brought home for his lunch some cheese which the grocer had wrapped in a page of the New Testament, which he was using for wrapping paper. After eating his lunch Qasim picked up the piece of paper and read the story of the man who hired laborers for his vineyard, and at the end of the day paid all the laborers the same wage, whether they had worked twelve hours or one. Qasim liked the story, and next day went again to the grocery store and bought cheese, asking that it be wrapped "in another page of that book." Finally, on the third day he bought what remained of the New Testament and showed it to his brother. The two of them then went to the missionary, who gave them a complete copy, and also gave them regular instruction in the Word of God. Both men were later baptized and were among the first believers in Meshed.

The Princess

Esmat-ul-Moluk (Virtue of Kings) was the granddaughter of one of the rulers of Iran, and the widow of the richest man in the country, whose favorite wife she had been. Her large home was near the campus of the Christian school for boys in Teheran, of which the famous missionary educator, Dr. Samuel Jordan, was the principal. When a question of water rights arose, which affected the property of both the princess and the school, Dr. and Mrs. Jordan went to call on Esmat-ul-Moluk to discuss the matter.

Mrs. Jordan, always eager to make Christ known to her pupils in the school and to her friends, invited Esmat to tea, and the two ladies became friends. She also invited the princess to go with her to a service in the Persian church, and Esmat liked it so much that she became a regular attendant. The services of worship, with singing and praying in Persian, not in Arabic as in the mosques, met her need. She heard the Good News of Christ, both from the preacher and from her Christian friend.

Once Mrs. Jordan said to me, "Do you know that there is a princess who comes regularly to church when you are preaching, and likes to hear the gospel?"

"No," I replied, "all those women sit there completely covered with their black veils, and I can't tell a princess from a beggar! I don't know whether they are listening, or laughing at me, or are asleep. I just preach to them, hoping that something will get through their veils to them!" Mrs. Jordan laughed and said, "Yes, she is really interested."

When I returned to Teheran after an absence Mrs. Jordan again mentioned the princess to me. "I think she has faith in Christ," she said. "You and Mrs. Miller should call on her and ask her if she does not want to be baptized and become a member of the church." So we made an appointment and called on Esmat. We received a warm welcome and were served tea and cakes and fruit, and enjoyed the kind of hospitality for which the people of Iran are famous. Then I told our hostess how happy we were that she attends church and likes to worship with Christians, and asked whether she did not want to become a Christian herself. "I have always been a Christian!" responded the princess. "I have loved Jesus Christ ever since I was a girl. Yes, I am ready to be baptized."

And so in due time, after she had been instructed and examined and approved for baptism, Esmat-ul-Moluk one Sunday morning came to the front of the room in which the service for Christians only was being held, pushed the veil back from her forehead, professed her faith in Christ, and received Christian baptism. It was a time of joy for her and for us all. God had used the love and prayers of a Christian friend to make the princess his child and a member of his family.

Esmat continued to come to church regularly until, because of financial difficulties, she had to move from her big house in the city to a very small house ten miles distant. Also her health became poor, and she was unable any longer to come to church. So her Christian friends visited her and read the Bible and prayed with her. She led a lonely life, for her relatives largely ignored her because she had become a Christian. The maids, who had been with her from her girlhood, now old and infirm like their mistress, took care of her.

We would sometimes take visitors to call on the princess, and they all received a cordial welcome. When the tea had been brought, Esmat would tell one of her maids to bring in her album, and would show the visitors a picture of herself when she was young, beautifully dressed and seated in a fine carriage. "That was my carriage, and those were my horses and my servants," she would say. "Yes, I once had clothes and jewels and everything —but I was not happy a single day. Now I am old and infirm and poor, but I am happy in Christ."

When Esmat-ul-Moluk died she was given a Muslim burial by her family, and her Christian friends were not informed of her death. A request to her daughter that permission be given to the church to hold a memorial service for her was refused. The family wanted to make it appear that she had never been a Christian. But one day the truth will appear, for, as Dr. Zwemer used to say, "On the Day of Resurrection many Christians will rise from Muslim graveyards!"

The Doctor Who Found Happiness

Young Dr. Norollah (Light of God) was an intern in the Christian hospital in Teheran. One day Dr. Hoffman, the missionary doctor, said to him, "Dr. Norollah, what is your religion?" "Please don't talk to me about religion," replied the young man, "I have no religion but the practice of medicine." He was counted as a Muslim, but like many of the educated young people he had no interest in religious matters. So Dr. Hoffman was unable to tell his friend about Jesus Christ.

While serving in the Christian hospital Dr. Norollah was deeply impressed by the fact that the American doctors really enjoyed their work. He thought that this was because they got good results from their work, and also had a good income. (He would have been surprised had he known how small was the salary of a missionary doctor!) He realized that he was not happy like these men. So he determined that he would become the head of a hospital, would get rich, and then attain to happiness.

Ten years passed, and Dr. Norollah acquired a good position and adequate income—but he still was not happy. So he decided to sell his practice and go to America to find the secret of happiness. In Boston, where he was studying, he began at the suggestion of a friend, to attend a Congregational church for the purpose of improving his English. One night at the mid-week service the minister spoke about happiness. He said that happiness could not be found through gaining position or wealth, but was the gift of Christ. Dr. Norollah was sure that the sermon was being preached at him, and he left the church in anger, not even speaking to the minister as he went past him at the door. But that night he had a dream which completely changed him. When he awoke he discovered that he had the happiness he had been seeking for so long. It was evident that this had come to him through the church. So he apologized to the minister, and asked for baptism. In due time he was baptized.

Dr. Norollah had thought of remaining in America. But he remembered his friends in Iran who like him were seeking happiness, and did not know where to find it. So he resolved to return to Teheran. I first met Dr. Norollah when he walked into my office one morning and told me his story.

He said, "Before I went to America I was so un-happy that I looked like a criminal. My face was so dark and evil that I was ashamed to have my picture taken. Now look at me!" Sure enough, the joy in his heart was shining in his radiant countenance. His old friends at once saw the difference, and asked, "What did you bring back from America that made you so happy, a medical degree, a fortune, or what?" "No," replied Dr. Norollah, "I found Christ in America. But you don't have to go there to become happy. Believe on Christ, and you will find here what I found in Boston."

The doctor's friends began to gather in his home once a week to hear his story and to learn more of Christ. Seeing the great change in him, and in the way in which he now treated his pa-tients with love and without covetousness, a num-ber of men professed faith in Christ, and were later baptized. It seemed as though this might be the beginning of a little "mass movement" toward Christianity, which could usher in a new day in evangelism in Iran. But sad to say it did not continue. The police became disturbed at the size of the weekly meetings in the home of the doctor, fearing that these gatherings had a politi-cal purpose. The men, on learning that they were being watched, ceased to come to the meetings. To our great distress, this promising beginning had a speedy end. "It seems that God doesn't want the people of Iran to become Christians," complained the discouraged doctor.

Dr. Norollah and those who had been baptized

continued for some time in the church, but finally they lost interest and became "inactive members." Perhaps they were like the people whom Jesus described in the parable as soil which had no depth, which received the good seed with joy. The seed sprouted and grew up quickly, but when the sun became hot it withered and died for lack of root (Matt. 13:5-6). But did these brothers of ours really "die"? Only God knows. Since they once boldly confessed Christ before men, we who love them hope that he will confess them before his Father, and that we will meet them again, if not in the church on earth, at last in the Father's House above.

A Christian Family

Hasan's teacher was a *sayyid,* a descendant of Muhammad, who had become a Christian. One day he said to Hasan, a bright teenager in his school, "Do you want to find the truth? If so, compare the Koran with the *Injil* (New Testament), and decide for yourself." Hasan did want to find the truth, so he set to work. Reading the New Testament was easy, for he had a copy in his mother tongue, which was Persian. Reading the Koran in Arabic, a foreign language, was more difficult. But Hasan persisted, recording his findings in two parallel columns headed "What the Koran Says" and "What the Injil Says." There were more contradictions than similarities. By the time Hasan had completed his study, he decided that the truth was in the *Injil,* and he believed on Christ.

There was no church and no missionary in the little town on the Caspian Sea where Hasan lived. But now and then the Rev. Harry Schuler from Teheran used to visit that region and see his old friend, Hasan's teacher. On one of these visits he baptized Hasan. Later Hasan was married. His wife was a Muslim and did not want to become a Christian, as her husband hoped she would do. Several children were born, and Dr. Schuler at Hasan's request baptized them. But their mother would not believe and be baptized.

Some years passed, and I had the opportunity to visit Hasan and his family, whom I had never seen. I learned that his wife was in bed recovering from a serious illness. When I asked about her health she said, "A wonderful thing happened to me. When I was very sick and the doctors feared I would not get well, Jesus Christ appeared to me and said, 'You will recover!' " From that time I began to get better, and now I am almost well."

"Praise God!" I said, "that was indeed a wondeful experience you had. Tell me, what do you now think of Jesus Christ?"

"He is the Savior," she replied, "he saved me from death!"

"Do you believe on him?" I asked.

"Of course I do," said she, "and I want to be baptized." In due time she was baptized in her own home, and the Nikpur family became a Christian family. Remembering that Hasan had been baptized by Dr. Schuler, and knowing how he would rejoice to hear that the wife and all the children had become Christians, I wrote to tell him the good news. Soon a reply came from Dr. Schuler, who had retired and was living in California. "How glad I am to hear of her baptism!" he wrote. "I prayed for that lady for twenty years!"

Later Hasan Nikpur came to Teheran, and was trained in the "School of Evangelism" to be an evangelist. He loved to sit in the Christian Reading Room, and talk to young men who came in to learn about Christ. He became gifted in writing personal letters to Muslim inquirers, explaining the Bible to them and answering their objections. He often went to other towns to sell literature and give his testimony, and he conducted a Bible correspondence course. Later he was ordained as a pastor.

In the case of this family, we see how God used the influence of a teacher, the study of the Bible and the Koran, the prayers and teaching of a missionary, the love and prayers of a husband and father, an illness and a dream and a remarkable healing, to accomplish his saving purpose. "Blessed be the Lord God . . . who only doeth wondrous things!" (Ps. 72:18).

The Artist

"This is my friend Husayn Behzad," said an Iranian Christian to me at the close of an evangelistic meeting in the Teheran Evangelical Church. "He needs Christ very much!" As he sat slouched down on a seat at the rear of the church, it was evident that Behzad was in real need of help. His friend had brought him to the meetings and had told him of Christ. Before long Behzad decided to become a Christian.

Behzad was a miniature painter. He could paint exquisite little pictures with lines and figures so small they could be clearly seen only with the help of a magnifying glass. But his life was being ruined by drugs and drink, and his Christian friend was able with the love and power of Christ to save him. He lived many years after his conversion, and became the best miniature artist in Iran. His wife also believed on Christ. Often I visited them in their little home, and all of us prayed together.

A Christian agency called "Lit-Lit," the purpose of which was to promote literacy and literature, invited Christian artists in other countries to submit paintings depicting the Nativity, the best of which would be used as a Christmas card. Behzad sent to New York his lovely painting of "Wise Men from the East," and in 1958 this received the award. It was most appropriate that a painting from Iran, the land from which the Wise Men came to Bethlehem, should have been chosen. Three hundred thousand copies of this picture were sold and distributed around the world. When in appreciation for this service a citation and a medal were presented to the artist, Behzad in reply said, "I have received many honors, but I count this greater than any other. For the others came from men, but this came from Jesus Christ." Another painting of Behzad's was used by Lit-Lit as the 1967 Christmas card. It was entitled "Persian

Magi," and was the most beautiful card I have ever seen.

I had a desire to present to Princeton Theological Seminary, from which I graduated, something from Iran as an expression of my gratitude for what I had there received. So I asked Behzad to prepare a pattern for a Persian rug or tapestry, which a Christian weaver whom I knew would weave. The pattern which Behzad painted was itself a beautiful work of art, and when the weaving was completed the rug was an exquisite creation. It represented Christ as the Good Shepherd holding lovingly in his arms a lamb which he had rescued from the dark mountain of sin, and was carrying back to the green pastures of paradise from which it had strayed. Beside the Shepherd was the tree of life, and the blossoms at the top of the tree formed a cross. From the hem of the robe of the Shepherd flowed a little stream of living water, and along the banks of the stream beautiful flowers were blooming. I have always felt that in this picture Behzad had related the story of his own salvation by the loving Shepherd. This rug is now hanging on the wall in a hall of Princeton Seminary, a reminder to all who see it that Jesus Christ came to seek and to save the lost, and that he bids his disciples to follow in his steps. Behzad's portrayal of the Seeking Shepherd was reproduced on the cover of the original edition of this book.

When Husayn Behzad died in 1968 he had a big funeral in a mosque in Teheran, and there were front-page articles about him in the Persian newspapers, but not a word was said about his having been a Christian. Without the salvation which Christ gave him he would never have lived to become Iran's famous artist. But in his case, as in that of many others, the Muslims wanted to deny and obliterate the truth that he was a Christian.

I was deeply hurt by this dishonor to our Lord and to our brother Behzad. So I was very grateful when the mission agency of our church undertook to prepare a filmstrip of Behzad's Christian paintings, of which there are a number. A narrative also was prepared which explained the pictures and told of the artist's faith in Christ.[3] This is a memorial to a Christian whose body lies in a Muslim graveyard. As we have seen, it was largely through the friendship of an Iranian Christian that Behzad found new life in Christ.

A Christian's Tears

"It was Mr. Wilson's tears that led me to become a Christian," said Abbas Abhari. Abbas was a Muslim cleric in the town of Damghan. When the Rev. Ivan Wilson, a missionary in Teheran, came to this little town and began to distribute Christian literature and talk with people about Christ, Abbas came one night to call on him. His purpose was not to become a Christian, or even to learn what the Christian teaching is, but to demonstrate the superiority of Islam to

[3] *Christ in the Art of Hussein Behzad of Iran* (United Presbyterian Church, 475 Riverside Drive, New York, N. Y.).

Christianity, and to humiliate the missionary.

Mr. Wilson talked kindly to the Muslim caller, and explained the doctrines of the Bible to him. But Abbas made the usual response. No, Jesus was not God's Son, he did not die on the cross, and he foretold the coming of Muhammad. Also the Christian Scriptures have been corrupted, and Christians worship three gods. The missionary patiently tried to explain the misunderstandings and answer the arguments of the Muslim, but all to no avail. Abbas began to feel very proud of himself that he had defeated the Christian teacher in argument, when he saw a strange sight. The missionary began to weep!

Several years passed, and other evangelists from Teheran visited Damghan. Then I was there on "World Communion Sunday," and a little service was conducted. There were two of us at the Lord's Table, the missionary and Abbas. After we had taken the bread and the cup and had prayed together, I said to Abbas, "My brother, what was it that led you to Christ?"

"Mr. Wilson's tears led me to Christ," replied Abbas.

"How was that?" I inquired, "I never heard of anyone's being made a Christian by tears."

"It was thus," replied my brother. "Mr. Wilson came here, he talked with me and argued with me, but I felt I had overcome him, and I was feeling very proud of myself. Then that man of God felt so sorry for me in my unbelief and pride that he began to weep. His tears did for me what his arguments did not do. They melted my heart, and

I believed and became a Christian. Later I was baptized."

On another visit to Damghan I had the joy of conducting a service of worship in the little home of Abbas. We sat in a circle on the floor, and the wife and six children were all baptized. What a day of joy it was for us all! God had used the message of the gospel and the heart-felt love of the missionary and the influence of the father to bring a whole family to faith in Christ.

I have related these stories of a few of the many hundreds of people in Iran who, during the past half-century, have professed faith in Christ as illustrations of how God's Spirit operates. Some of them were poor and some were rich, some were old and some were young, some highly educated and others illiterate, some were pious Muslims who said the daily prayers and kept the month of fasting, and others had lost all faith and interest in Islam. And God, for whom nothing is impossible, led them by various means to Christ, the one true Way to God the Father. When I am asked how many Muslims I converted in Iran, I always reply, "I never converted anyone. Some became Christians, but God did it, not I." To God be the glory!

7
Presenting the Gospel to Muslims

PRESENTING THE GOSPEL TO MUSLIMS

Some of the readers of this little book may be missionaries who long to tell the Good News of Christ to Muslims in their own lands and in their mother tongues. Other readers may be faithful followers of Christ who have not been called of God to become foreign missionaries, but who desire to support by their gifts and their informed intercession all efforts to evangelize Muslims. And others will perhaps find themselves in communities in their own country in which Muslim immigrants or visitors are in residence. The suggestions made in this chapter regarding the presentation of the gospel to the people of Islam are intended for all who desire the salvation of Muslims.

Become Acquainted with Muslims and with Islam

First of all, to influence Muslims one must know them. If we are in personal touch with them, we must remember that they are people like us, with their joys and sorrows, their burdens and anxieties, their fears and their hopes, their failures and their sins. We should seek to know them so well that they will trust us, and will open their hearts and tell us their deepest needs. We should also know their customs and their beliefs. Christians serving in Muslim lands should, if possible, learn the native language well. At Pentecost God caused each person present in Jerusalem to hear the Good News of salvation in his own tongue, and those who have been used of God in leading Muslims to Christ have usually been those who were able to speak God's message accurately and effectively in Arabic and Persian and Turkish and Urdu and the other Muslim languages. This is less important when the Muslim knows English well, as many do.

Also, the Christian should become well acquainted with the history and doctrines and practices of Islam. Only when he knows Islam well will he be able to present Christian truth in a way that will be intelligible and attractive to Muslims, and be able to avoid misunderstandings. For example, the Muslim may ask his Christian friend, "Do you believe in God's prophets?" If the answer is "yes," the Muslim will understand that to mean that the Christian agrees with him that God has sent 124,000 prophets into the world, all of them sinless, the last and greatest being Muhammad. This is not exactly the Christian doctrine of prophethood! Everyone concerned about the evangelization of Muslims should read at least a part of the Koran in a translation, and also several of the excellent books on Islam listed in the Bibliography. If the Christian shows that he is ignorant of Islam, can he expect the Muslim to take him seriously when he attempts to show that Christianity is God's best gift to the world?

Love the People of Islam

In the second place, Christians who would draw Muslims to Christ must not only know them and their beliefs, but must also love them. This reminder is necessary, for it is easy to think of Muslims as enemies to be overcome rather than as lost children of God to be sought and saved. We know that Islam has for 1,300 years denied the basic truths of Christ's deity, his death on the cross for sinners, his resurrection, and his finality, and has pushed him off the throne to seat another in his place. It is not surprising that zealous Christians eight hundred years ago launched the Crusades to break the power of Muslim rule and deliver the Holy Land. They hated the "infidels," and slew them with the sword, contrary to the command of Christ, till they were finally defeated by them.

We today agree that this was a tragic mistake, which planted seeds of bitterness which remain in the Middle East till now. We would never want to fight Islam with sword or bomb. However, as we hate and fight against the false teachings of Islam with spiritual weapons, Satan may tempt us to hate also the people who hold these doctrines and who dishonor our Lord Jesus. We may desire so much to see them defeated in argument that we are tempted to put more importance on the triumph of truth than on the salvation of sinners. As representatives of him who prayed for his murderers, we while hating all heresy must in obedience to our Master love these opponents of the gospel. When converts are asked what first drew them to Christ, it often appears that the means most used of God has been the Christ-like love of Christians. This love is not an emotional attraction, for the people we are to love often are, but may not always be, lovable. It is the kind of love described in the thirteenth chapter of First Corinthians, the kind of love revealed in Christ on the cross. It is love that is ready to give life not only for friends but also for enemies.

Once when I was in Egypt I had the privilege of meeting a famous convert and a great servant of God whose name was Sheikh Kamal Mansur. When a young man Kamal had been a student in the great Muslim theological school, Al-Azhar. Once he and a group of fanatical students had invaded a Christian church in Cairo and with their own hands had broken up the pulpit. The brother of Kamal, who had previously become a Christian, was serving Christ in this church. The police rushed in and arrested the zealous Muslim youths, among them Kamal Mansur. Then his brother came out and pleaded with the police, saying he was young and inexperienced.

Kamal was accordingly released by the police, but he soon found himself a prisoner of the love of Christ. He could not understand how his brother, whom he and the other men wanted to beat and perhaps to kill for becoming a Christian, could thus forgive him and secure his release. In time he too became a Christian, and a preacher. "When I first preached in the church," he told me,

"I was reminded that the pulpit from which I was preaching the gospel was the very one I had helped once to destroy!" Was it not Paul's love that led him to say of the Jews who wanted to kill him, "My heart's desire and prayer to God for them is that they may be saved"? A godly teacher in Cambridge University who led many of his students to Christ once wrote, "To influence you must love, and to love, you must pray."[1]

Pray Without Ceasing

In the task of evangelizing Muslims, prayer is essential. This is a task too great for man, but not for God. It is to God that those whose heart's desire is the salvation of Muslims are continually turning. It was Christ himself who told his disciples that they would be able by faith in God to move mountains, and he added, "Whatever you ask in prayer, believe that you receive it, and you will" (Mark 11:23-24). And again he said, "If two of you agree on earth about anything they ask, it will be done for them by my Father in heaven" (Matt. 18:19). We cannot move the mighty mountains of difficulty that have hindered the progress of the gospel, but God can and will do it. So we cry out to him in ceaseless prayer.

We will pray for ourselves and for all Christians on whose hearts God has laid the burden of Islam, that our faith may not fail. This was the prayer of the Lord for his weak disciple Peter (Luke 22:32), and it was abundantly answered.

---

[1] Forbes Robinson, *Letters to His Friends* (New York: Longmans, Green and Co., 1911), p. 164.

As we meet discouragements and heartbreaking disappointments day after day, Satan desires to "sift" us as he wished to do with Peter, and to undermine our faith in God and his saving purpose for Muslims. This is why we must "pray constantly" (I Thess. 5:17). Certainly the fidelity of many of Christ's servants, who have labored on for years in the Muslim world in joy and hope without seeing any adequate results, is due to their own prayers and to the prevailing intercession of their friends. If some lost hope and gave up the task, may it not have been because of their failure and the failure of their supporters to use the powerful weapon of "all-prayer" (Eph. 6:18) in the battle against the tempter?

Prayer also must be offered to the Lord of the harvest that he will send forth laborers to tell the Good News to Muslims (Matt. 9:38). As has been noted, the number of trained and Spirit-filled witnesses for Christ among the Muslims of the world is utterly inadequate, and most Muslims have never once heard the message about Jesus Christ. No one should become a missionary to Muslims unless God has chosen and equipped him for this difficult task. Whether he or she be a member of one of the great churches in the East and in Africa, or a Christian from the West, a divine appointment is essential.

But why does God not raise up and send forth more apostles for the evangelization of Muslims? Is it not his will that all men should hear the gospel? Perhaps the paucity of laborers is because of the failure of God's people to pray, and we know that the calling of men and women to this service is frequently God's answer to prevailing intercession. On April 10, 1916, at the very hour when Dr. Zwemer and a group of Christians were meeting in the New York home of Mrs. Borden to pray that God would send someone to the Muslims of China in the place of her son William, who had died in Cairo, a young man named George K. Harris in Chicago received the conviction, as he was in prayer about his future work, that God had called him to this unoccupied and needy field. He obeyed, and became a powerful witness to Christ in China and Southeast Asia. He did not learn till later that his call to China came to him at the very time of the prayer meeting in New York.[2] Oh that God would raise up a host of men and women in all lands to make Christ known by word and deed throughout the whole Muslim world!

Those who are in personal touch with Muslims will of course pray for them by name, that they may be saved. Before talking with them, while with them, after the conversation, and in the days and weeks to follow, their "heart's desire and prayer to God" for them will be that they will believe on Christ. How long should one pray for the conversion of people who do not seem to respond? Certainly as long as God lays their need on one's heart!

Once in Teheran a devout Christian physician

[2] Malcolm R. Bradshaw, *Torch for Islam: Biography of G. K. Harris* (Overseas Missionary Fellowship, 1965), pp. 26-27.

named Dr. Ibrahim, the nephew of the famous Dr. Sa'eed Khan, came to me in great excitement. "Come quickly and baptize my mother!" he said. "I have prayed for fifty years that she would believe on Christ and be baptized, and now at last she is ready." And so on the following afternoon I went to the home of the doctor with several elders of the church. There was his mother, more than ninety years of age, nicely dressed and seated in a chair, ready to be baptized. She had become so deaf that I had to shout the questions into her ear. "Do you believe in Christ as your Savior? Do you want to be baptized in his name?" "Yes, yes!" she replied. And I had the joy of putting the water of baptism on her head. But how great was the joy of her son, who had kept on praying till he received what he had asked! Several years later the mother went to be with the Lord, and now her son has joined her in the Father's House. What a joyous reunion he must have had with his parents, both converts from Islam!

When the Muslim believer is baptized the need for prayer for him does not end. Perhaps it is greater than ever, for Satan will most certainly try to recapture those who have escaped from his power. The new convert will probably meet persecution and all sorts of difficulties as he carries his cross after Christ. He must be encouraged to pray constantly for himself, and his Christian brethren must support him continually by their love and prayers.

Not only should prayer be offered for individuals, we should pray also for nations and their rulers. There are lands which no Christian missionary is permitted to enter, and lands in which conversion to Christianity is forbidden by law, and in which a convert might soon become a martyr. For many years believing prayer has been offered for these lands, that closed doors and closed minds and hearts might be opened to the truth, and in some cases these prayers have been wonderfully answered. But in many other cases those who prayed "died in faith not having received what was promised, but having seen it and greeted it from afar" (Heb. 11:13). We who continue to pray await eagerly the day when "great and effectual doors" will be opened everywhere, and multitudes of Muslims will hear the Good News and believe on Christ.

As a result of hearing a passionate plea made by Dr. Zwemer in the Keswick Conference in England in 1915, a group of praying Christians decided to form the "Fellowship of Faith for the Muslims," for the purpose of promoting prayer and effort for the salvation of the people of Islam. In 1952 a North American branch of the Fellowship was established in Toronto.[3] Prayer bulletins are provided for those who wish to pray intelligently for all parts of the Muslim world, prayer meetings are arranged, and information regarding needs and opportunities is supplied. Various missions which have work in Muslim lands publish prayer requests and encourage the formation of prayer groups. But the Church of Christ around

[3] Fellowship of Faith for Muslims, Room 25, 205 Yonge Street, Toronto, Canada M5B 1N2

the world has not really taken on its heart the salvation of these 800 million of our fellowmen for whom Christ died. No doubt the greatest lack in the work of evangelizing Muslims is that of "effectual fervent prayer" (James 5:16). Even Christians who have never seen Muslims are able by prayer to help effectively in saving them.

Teach the Bible to Inquirers

How does one tell the Good News to Muslims? There is no fixed pattern. Each person is different, and each must be approached in the way most appropriate for him. As a result of friendship and conversation with a Christian, or the reading of Christian literature, or something else that God has used to influence him, a Muslim may express a desire to understand Christianity better. Then the most important thing to do is to help him to read and understand the Bible. If it is possible, a Christian should read the Bible with him, and give him the many explanations which will be necessary. Because of cultural attitudes, it is preferable that Muslim women be assisted in such study by Christian women, and men by men. It is good to begin the study with one of the Gospels, so that the inquirer will learn who Jesus really is and claimed to be. If there is a class in which his need will be met, he should be encouraged to join it, and have fellowship with other seekers and believers. In Iran there were in some places Bible study groups meeting every night to which interested young men used to come, and a number of them as a result professed faith in Christ.

In recent years it has been found that Bible correspondence schools are able to give instruction to many thousands of Muslims in various countries, most of whom have been young people who live far from a Christian church, or who prefer to study at home rather than to face possible trouble by going openly to a Christian center. Likewise, much Christian instruction is being given by radio, and many who hear the messages write for literature or enroll in a correspondence course. Thus God is using the posts and the radio to bring his message to multitudes of Muslims who otherwise would never have heard.

Receive Believers into Christian Fellowship

We learn from the New Testament that those who heard and believed the gospel were baptized and became members of God's Family, the Church. They were not left as isolated believers in Christ, but were united by the Holy Spirit as members of one Body. It is especially important that converts from Islam, cut off as they probably will be from their families and their Islamic community, be received as beloved members of a Christian church. It sometimes happens in certain situations that a convert will feel a strong attachment for his Christian teacher, whom he trusts, but will not want to be related to other converts, whom he does not trust, because he fears they may be spies. Till the believer publicly professes his faith in baptism and becomes a member of the Body of Christ, loving and trusting the other members, he is not a complete Christian. It is often in the

Christian group that an inquirer sees the truth and love and joy of Christ, and decides to take up the cross and confess Christ before men, whatever the cost may be.

Make Clear What It Means to Be a Christian

In welcoming Muslims who express a desire to profess faith in Christ and become Christians, it is necessary to follow the example of our Lord and not assume that every expression of faith is real. We are told that in Jerusalem "many believed in his name . . . but Jesus did not trust himself to them, because he knew all men" (John 2:23-25). We do not have that knowledge of men's hearts and motives. But we should remember that in Muslim lands the "convenient lie" is not considered an offense. It is thought better to tell such lies than to speak words of truth that cause trouble or even unhappiness. Hence, when a Muslim knows that his Christian friend is very desirous that he become a Christian, he may to please his friend, or for some other purpose, profess a faith which he does not possess.

Also, when the Muslim says he believes in Christ, he may from his own point of view be speaking the truth. For he does "believe" in Christ, just as he believes in Noah and Ishmael and Job and all the other prophets. But he may not yet have put his sole trust in Christ the Son of God for his salvation. So when a Muslim makes a profession of faith in Christ his Christian friend should rejoice, but not assume that he has now become a real Christian. He must be helped to understand clearly what it is to be a Christian, what it may cost him, and what in the future his relation to Islam must be. Christians may be so eager to have their prayers answered, and to see their Muslim friends saved, that they will be tempted to put undue pressure on them to "give their hearts to Christ." They may not yet have sufficient knowledge of who Christ is to submit to him. Or, even if they know Christ truly, they may not yet have counted the cost, as Jesus commanded all to do (Luke 14:26-33). Is the new believer ready to lose his home, his support, his opportunity to get a good job and a promotion, the esteem of his family and friends, and even his life, for Christ's sake? It is not for a missionary to tell a Muslim that he should take a step that might cost him his life, for only the Holy Spirit is qualified to do this. The Spirit has often done it in the past in all lands, and will do it again in the case of everyone who has been chosen by God for salvation.

In obedience to the command of Christ, believers should be baptized. But the question arises, when should a convert from Islam be baptized? Should baptism immediately follow a profession of faith in Christ, or should it be delayed and follow a period of instruction and testing? When the man from Ethiopia professed faith, Philip baptized him in the first stream of water they came to in their journey (Acts 8:26-39). And on the same memorable night when the prison in Philippi was shaken by the earthquake, Paul baptized the jailer and his household who had just believed on Christ (Acts 16:25-34). Following the examples of these early missionaries, I in my early years in Iran baptized a number of Muslims who, in the remote villages I visited, had professed faith in Christ. Later I was rebuked by an elder in the Teheran Evangelical Church, himself a convert from Islam, where the rule was that those who professed faith should receive at least a year of training before being baptized. I said to the elder, whose opinion I highly respected, "But didn't Philip baptize the Ethiopian immediately?" "Yes," he said, "but you are not Philip!" That was true.

I had thought that converts were often discouraged by the long delay of baptism, and that receiving baptism would strengthen them as they undertook to live as Christians in places where there was no church and no spiritual fellowship. But in places where the new believer could receive regular instruction and share in the fellowship of older believers, it had been thought wise to delay baptism. Which course is preferable? Probably most of those who were speedily baptized by me fell away and did not finish the course. But there have also been many whom I knew who had to wait for months for baptism who likewise failed to reach the goal. No general rule can be adhered to. But certainly the applicant for baptism should first understand who Christ is, and what faith in Christ means, and what his responsibilities as a Christian will be, and should show in his life that he has indeed been born again.

Introduce Converts to a Church
Which Will Welcome Them

In places where the members of the Christian churches are from an ethnic background different from that of the Muslims, and may not wish for various reasons to welcome converts into their fellowship, it may be very difficult for the convert to find a spiritual home. How should this problem be solved? We know that in Christ there is neither Jew nor Greek, neither Turk nor Armenian, and God wishes all who have become his children through Christ to be members of his Family, which is the Church, where all will be one. This unity will be a powerful testimony to the world that Christ is indeed from God (John 17:21).

In some countries Christians have earnestly endeavored to bring together in one church all believers from different races and cultures and languages, and to encourage the older Christians to welcome new believers from Islam. Sometimes this effort has met with success, but often it has failed. Accordingly, some evangelists to Muslims now advocate the formation of new churches composed largely of converts. Though such churches may not witness clearly to the oneness of all believers in Christ, it is probable that they will be able to attract and to hold more believers from Islam than the older churches have done. Such churches composed of new believers will of course for a time lack the experience of mature Christians, and may have the same kind of problems as those which arose in the church in Corinth in Paul's day.

Emphasize What Is Unique in the Gospel

The question is sometimes asked, "In presenting Christianity to Muslims, should one emphasize the similarities or the differences? Certainly it is well, at least at the beginning, for the Christian to assure the Muslim that he agrees with him in the belief that God is one, and that he alone should be worshiped. He may also remind the Muslim that they both believe that Jesus was born of the Virgin Mary, and that he is alive in heaven today. Also, both Christians and Muslims are aware that they have sinned and need God's forgiveness. And other similarities may be mentioned to establish a friendly understanding. However, emphasizing the likenesses will lead the Muslim to say, "We are really one, so why talk about the things that have divided us? We who believe in God should unite in opposing atheistic communism!" It is improbable that this approach will ever lead a Muslim to become a Christian.

Then what is it that has induced Muslims to renounce the religion of Islam, and put their trust in Christ alone for salvation? It is not the similarities but the great differences between the gospel of Christ and the religion that has Mecca as its center. It is the difference between faith in a loving Father in heaven, who like the good shepherd seeks for the one who is lost till he finds it, and submission to the unpredictable will of an all-powerful God who is unlike anything that one can imagine, and is therefore unknowable; between putting one's trust for salvation and forgiveness in God's Son who died as a sacrifice for sinners, and attempting to save oneself by doing works of merit, which will never be enough to cancel one's sins; between following a living Lord who conquered death by rising from the tomb on the third day and is with his disciples always, and making a pilgrimage to the grave of a man who died more than 1,300 years ago and whose tomb is not empty; between the possibility of living a pure and holy life in the power of the Holy Spirit, and struggling in one's own strength to overcome sin and Satan and live a life pleasing to a holy God; between having as one's example and guide the sinless Son of God, and the "Prophet" from Mecca who, according to the Koran, was only a man like other men, and was commanded by God to repent of his sins; between facing death with the assurance of immediate entrance into the Father's House to be forever in the holy presence of Christ, and undergoing the terrifying questioning of the two angels, and the possibility of final entrance into the fires of hell. The realization of these and other basic differences between the two religions has caused not a few sincere seekers for God to choose the "Pearl of Great Price," whatever the cost might be (Matt. 13:45).

Avoid Controversy Whenever Possible

The question here arises as to whether the controversy with Muslims is a proper form of

Christian witness. In the past it was sometimes possible in certain countries to arrange public debates in which learned representatives of Islam and Christianity would discuss the merits of the two faiths. These discussions of course aroused much interest in religious matters, and it sometimes happened that people in the audience were convinced of the truth of Christianity and later believed in Christ. However, there was always danger that the defenders of the gospel might lose their tempers on hearing what the Muslims said, or might speak unkind words to their opponents which might drive them yet further away from the truth and love of Christ.

Such public discussions are usually unwise and impossible today, since there is lack of religious freedom in most of the Muslim countries. However, when a Muslim in conversation with a Christian insists that Jesus was not crucified, that the Bible has been corrupted by Christians and is not trustworthy, and that Jesus foretold the coming of Muhammad, it is obligatory for the Christian in the spirit of love to give a reason for his faith, as it is written: "Always be prepared to make a defence to anyone who calls you to account for the hope that is in you, yet do it with gentleness and reverence" (I Peter 3:15). This may lead to a controversy, but the result may be deliverance of the Muslim from misunderstanding and error. We know that both Jesus Christ and Paul engaged in such controversy with those who opposed them.

However, in preaching in public meetings at

which Muslims are prsent, as well as in private conversation with Muslims, it is better to avoid all mention of Islam, of Muhammad, and of the Koran. If Islam is criticized by the Christian, unnecessary opposition may be aroused. If Islam is commended, the impression will be made that the Christian is really a Muslim at heart. The Christian teacher or preacher must know what the Muslim believes, and must try to state the full Christian message in the way least offensive to him. He will emphasize the Christian doctrines which Islam lacks or denies, and will thus try to correct the Muslim's misunderstandings and errors. Then if questions arise and objections are raised, they should be discussed in private conversation. In all these things Christians need to be "wise as serpents and innocent as doves," and continually obedient to the guidance of the Holy Spirit, who would speak through them (Matt. 10:16-20).

In the past some very powerful books were written to demonstrate to Muslims the inadequacy of their faith. One of these was entitled *The Balance of Truth,* and was written by a German missionary, Dr. C. G. Pfander, who served Christ nearly a century and a half ago in the Middle East and in India. It was published in Persian and Arabic and English[4] and probably in other languages, and produced an angry response

---

[4] Recently republished in Arabic and English in Beirut. Copies may be secured from Fellowship of Faith for Muslims, Room 25, 205 Yonge St., Toronto, Canada M5B 1N2

from Muslims. However, it profoundly influenced a number of men, who became outstanding Christians. It appears that the age of controversy was blessed by the conversion of more great men than has been the present age of dialogue and conciliation.

Confess Christ As the Spirit Directs

When Jesus healed the leper, he forbade him to tell what had been done for him, but the man could not refrain from speaking (Mark 1:40-45). When the man with a legion of demons was delivered, Jesus said to him: "Go home to your friends, and tell them how much the Lord has done for you, and how he has had mercy on you" (Mark 5:19). In some situations a new believer should boldly and joyfully give his testimony, both by word and by deed, and invite others to believe on Christ. When he is able to do so, this confession of his faith will greatly strengthen him as it blesses others, and his testimony may have a greater influence than that of an older Christian. However, there are situations in which it may be wrong for the convert to profess his faith before people who would injure or even kill him. One should in no circumstances deny Christ (Matt. 10:33), and should confess him with his lips when and where he is guided to do so by the Holy Spirit. But in every situation the believer will be able by the new life of purity and honesty and love and service which he lives, to demonstrate that he has indeed experienced a "new birth." His actions may speak more loudly and more clearly than his words would have done, and those who see the change in him will seek to know the reason. He will then, of course, give the honor to his Savior (Rom. 10:9-10).

The Christian friends of a new believer naturally rejoice over his conversion, and are eager to tell the good news to others, or to report it in a Christian journal. But it is often essential that they should refrain from doing so, lest such notoriety bring spiritual or physical harm to the convert, or put the presence and work of Christians in his country in jeopardy.

Other suggestions for Christians who desire to lead their Muslim friends to faith in Christ are found in the small book *Your Muslim Guest* (see the Bibliography).

8

Duties are Ours, Results are God's

DUTIES ARE OURS, RESULTS ARE GOD'S

If a farmer has two fields, one of which is very productive, and the other because of its stony soil has never produced a large crop, in which will he sow his seed? Naturally, in the field which is fruitful. This is what Christian missionaries usually have done as they have undertaken the evangelization of the world. Certain peoples have proved to be very responsive to the gospel, and evangelists have labored in those fields with remarkable success. During the past half-century many millions of people in Korea and India and Africa and Latin America and other lands have joyfully received the Good News from the tens of thousands of Christians, national and foreign, who have witnessed there to Christ.

But what of the unresponsive peoples of the world, the Jews, the high-caste peoples in India, and the Muslims? Few laborers have served God in these fields, and the number of converts to Christianity has been proportionately small. In the past this procedure was probably the result not of an adopted policy, but of a natural tendency to follow the line of least resistance. Missionaries from the West were eager to see results, and to bear much fruit, as Christ commanded, and usually volunteered to go to places where there would be many baptisms. The unresponsive areas were passed by, not so much because of policy, but through neglect.

However, a few years ago this procedure was advocated as a missionary policy for the World Church. It was said that in some parts of the world the churches were "static" and were not growing. In other places large groups of people, even whole tribes, were moving toward Christianity, and churches were experiencing phenomenal growth. It was suggested that in these situations the Holy Spirit was working in power, and missionaries should be sent to such places to share in the ingathering. But they should not be sent in large numbers to serve where the churches were not growing, and where their efforts would be fruitless. It was even suggested that in such areas one or two missionaries from abroad as links with the World Church might be assigned for every four thousand church members.

When I heard of this new philosophy of missions I was deeply disturbed. What would this mean for Iran, where I was serving, and where the number of Protestant church members was not more than 4,000? Two Protestant missionaries in a land of many millions of Muslims! Could this be God's plan for the evangelization of the people of Iran? The same situation existed in other Muslim lands, and the adoption of this policy would have meant the end of almost all efforts on the part of missionaries from abroad to assist the small national churches in making Christ known to the huge Muslim populations among whom they lived. Fortunately this policy was not approved by most of the missionary agencies operating in Muslim areas.

However, I was recently surprised and distressed when a Christian American, who occupies an important position in the planning of missionary outreach, spoke to me after I had made an appeal in a meeting of pastors for the evangelization of Muslims. He said to me, "Why not take all missionaries out of Iran, and place them in productive areas? Think how many millions of dollars the Presbyterian Church has spent in that country during the past 140 years, and how disappointing has been the result!" There may be Christians who share this concern, and who are asking the question, "Is the effort to convert Muslims justified? Perhaps God does not want to save them."

And so as good stewards of God's resources it is our duty to give careful consideration to this matter. Can the expenditure of so much of God's money and of missionary life be justified, and should the effort to make disciples of Muslims be continued, however disappointing the results may be? I wish to state my convictions as I look back over more than half a century of deep involvement in Christian effort for Muslims. I believe that it is imperative that the Christian witness to Muslims in all the world be continued and greatly strengthened for many reasons, some of which I will now state.

1. Because of God's Love

The Good News of Christ must be made known to Muslims because they constitute a large part of the "world" which God loved so much that he gave his Son to save it. God loved and loves not only the children of Israel but also the children of Ishmael, not only the Jews but also the Muslim Gentiles. But how few of the people of Islam know how much God loves them! To us Christians has been given the glorious privilege and responsibility of making known to them by word and deed the wonders of God's love. If we fail in this duty Muslims will continue to live and die without truly knowing God.

2. Because of the Great Commission of Christ

Christians must make the gospel known to Muslims because our Lord Jesus Christ commanded them to do so. He commissioned his Church to preach the gospel to everybody in the world (Mark 16:15), and to make disciples of all nations (Matt. 28:19). Surely this command includes the one-sixth of the world's population who profess the religion of Islam. As loyal servants of Christ we dare not disobey his orders. We must make him known to the Muslims, as well as to all others in the world who do not know and obey him.

Sometimes it is said that Muslims have rejected the gospel, and we should therefore shake the dust from our feet and leave them to perish in unbelief (Matt. 10:14). But have they rejected the

Good News? Some have indeed done so. But the great majority of the 800 million Muslims now living in the world have not rejected the Christian message, for they have not yet heard it. Only when the gospel has been adequately made known so that every individual has had an opportunity to hear and accept it, can it truly be said that Muslims have rejected God's offer of salvation.

Also it must be remembered that in the spiritual as in the physical world, reaping follows plowing and sowing, and the plowman and the sower have just as important a part to play in producing a crop as has the reaper. When the day of harvest comes the sower and the reaper will rejoice together (John 4:36-38). God sometimes acts contrary to his usual plan, and produces a harvest as soon as the seed is sown. But he generally does his work more gradually, "first the blade, then the ear, then the full grain in the ear" (Mark 4:28). Seldom does it happen that a great spiritual harvest is reaped without a long preparation of preaching, witnessing, loving, serving, and praying.

3. Because of Christ's Love

Paul tells us that he and the other apostles were constrained by Christ's love to them to beseech men to be reconciled to God. Even if Christ had not commanded his followers to make disciples of all nations, his amazing love to them would have impelled them to give to Jews and Gentiles the gospel which had brought salvation to them.

Christ had died for them, and they could not rest until they had shown their gratitude by telling the world of him. The divine love which carried Paul all across the Roman world constrains Christians today to go to every part of the Muslim world and tell the Good News of Christ.

4. Because of the Second Great Commandment

When asked what the greatest commandment of God is, Jesus replied that it is to love God with one's whole being, and the second commandment is to love one's neighbor as oneself (Matt. 22: 37-40). To us Christ is the most precious treasure in the world. If we love our Muslim neighbors as ourselves, be they in America or Arabia, must we not do everything in our power to let them know that this priceless treasure has been given by God to them also? Christ is the Bread of Life. How can we eat and be satisfied, and fail to share this heavenly manna with our Muslim neighbors? To do so would be breaking God's great commandment, or else we would be agreeing with some of the Jews in Jesus' day that Muslims, like Samaritans, are not our neighbors.

5. Because of the Inadequacy of Islam

If, as some claim, Islam were adequate to meet the moral and spiritual needs of mankind, there would be no reason for trying to convert Muslims to Christianity. However, Islam is not adequate, as many of the converts to Christianity have testified. It fails to diagnose man's condition as a sinner unable to know and obey God perfectly, it fails to reveal God in his holiness and his love for sinful men, it fails to provide a Savior from sin and death, it fails to give the sinner assurance of forgiveness and peace with God, and it fails to supply the Holy Spirit to teach and guide and sanctify the believer. It points men to a dead prophet and not to the Lord Christ, who conquered death and is alive with us forever. Muslims need Jesus Christ just as much as do idol-worshipers in Africa or atheists in America.

6. Because of Islam's Denial of Truth

Christ appointed his disciples to be witnesses to him (Acts 1:8), and wherever he and his gospel are misrepresented or attacked they have the obligation to testify to the truth. This is what Stephen and Paul did in Jewish synagogues, and it is what Christians must do today by their holy lives, as well as by word and pen, in their contacts with Muslims. Islam, sad to say, denies the most important doctrines of the Bible. It denies that Jesus is the Son of God and one with his Father, that Jesus died on the cross and rose from the dead, that he is the one Savior of the world, the one Way to God the Father, and the Judge of the living and the dead. It falsely affirms that Jesus foretold the coming of Muhammad, who took his place as God's prophet on earth, and is superior to him.

Even if Christians are in a position where there is nothing else they can do, they must take their stand, even "to the end of the earth," as witnesses to the truth and love and supremacy of their Lord. When asked why he was giving his life in a most unresponsive area of the Middle East, the great missionary Dr. John Van Ess replied, "I am there for the honor of the Lord Jesus Christ." He was Christ's witness in a place where the supremacy and finality of Christ were being denied.

7. Because of the Resurgence of Islam

Another reason why the Christian witness to Muslims must be strengthened is that Islam is today being revived and has become more aggressive than in the past century. Though this revival is being stimulated chiefly for political reasons, and not for the salvation of souls, it is of concern to Christians who desire that Muslims be saved from sin. Not only are strenuous efforts being made by some Muslim governments and agencies to resist the influence of Christian missionaries, but the missionary outreach of Islam is being intensified. In African countries Islamic schools and hospitals and mosques have been established, there are Islamic broadcasts, and pagans and Christians are being converted. This is true also in other continents. The former Christian Cathedral in Libya is now said to be the "Islamic Conversion Centre." Mosques and Islamic centers are being built with oil income in Europe and America. The conversion of Westerners to Islam is being widely proclaimed. Islam is a missionary religion, and Christians must meet this religious *jihad* by a bold and loving proclamation of Christ both to Muslims and to those whom they would turn away from the truth.

8. Because of God's Working
in the Muslim World

A cause for encouragement in the task of evangelizing Muslims is the evidence of the working of God in various ways in the world of Islam. As the Roman roads made possible the travels of the early apostles across the Roman Empire, so the amazing development of the means of transportation and communication during the past half-century has made it possible for Christ's servants to go quickly to localities formerly too remote to be reached. The development of postal services has made possible the reaching of many people by Bible correspondence courses. The many Christian radio programs in Muslim languages go into lands closed to missionaries. Gospel recordings are being provided for hundreds of Muslim languages and dialects. The great improvement in education has made it possible for many millions of Muslims to read the Bible and Christian literature, which are being made available by the Bible societies and Christian publishers. And the Wycliffe Bible translators are busily engaged in reducing to writing and translating the Bible into languages spoken by Muslims as well as others who have never heard the Word of God. Truly God's hand is in all these achievements of science and education in Muslim lands.

Also in the providence of God some of the Muslim nations in recent years have wanted help from other countries in carrying out their extensive plans for development. Thousands of teachers, engineers, technicians, agricultural experts, and many others from the West and also from other lands have been recruited for such service. Among them have been Christian men and women, who have been able to reside and give a quiet Christian testimony by the quality of their lives, if not always by words, in lands still tightly closed to professional missionaries. What an opportunity for lay Christians, earning their own living, to render useful service to needy peoples, and to love and pray for those among whom they reside!

Though missionaries from the West are not permitted to reside in some of the Muslim countries, there are other lands the doors to which God has kept open, and in which they are able to serve unhindered and effectively. Many more missionaries are needed in these lands. And to some of the countries closed to Western missionaries their fellow-workers from Asia and Africa are able to gain admittance. Also, God is renewing by his Holy Spirit some of the ancient churches in the Middle East, and is laying on the hearts of members of these churches their responsibility for the salvation of their Muslim neighbors whom in the past they have largely neglected. These Christians, when filled with the love of Christ, are able to witness more effectively than any others to the Muslims among whom they live.

Moreover, God has brought to Europe and America hundreds of thousands of Muslim workers and business people and students and government agents who today are found in most of our cities and colleges. Many of them know English, they are ready to respond to sincere friendship, and some of them would like to know more about Christ. Formerly a missionary to Muslims had to go overseas and learn a foreign language, but now many Christians have become missionaries to Muslims in their own homes.

9. Because of the Value of Every Individual

Christians must continue to pray and labor for the salvation of Muslims because of the value in God's sight of every man, woman, and child whom he has created. It is sometimes erroneously supposed that missionary effort is justified only when large numbers of people are converted. Certainly Christ desires the salvation of "the great multitude which no man could number" (Rev. 7:9). But he also, like the shepherd, is ready to go after the one lost sheep and bring it home rejoicing. And he said that there was joy also in heaven over one sinner who repents. What is the worth of one child of God? He is worth the blood of the Son of God; he is of inestimable value! Then if only one Muslim were saved as a result of a century of Christian effort, would not this effort have been more than justified?

In Iran a century ago there was a proud and zealous Kurdish *mulla* (Muslim cleric) named Sa'eed, who became a humble and fearless Christian physician, and who rendered great service to the poor and also to the rich and great in his country. Regarding him Sir Mortimer Durand, once British minister in Teheran, volunteered this testimony: "If in all the years of its activities the American [Presbyterian] Mission had achieved nothing more than the conversion of Dr. Sa'eed, then its labors had been amply repaid."[1] Of course the missionaries would have replied, "It was God that did it, not we!" Whether the believer becomes a famous physician, or a faithful and humble follower of Christ, whose holy life is unheralded, he is "the brother for whom Christ died" (I Cor. 8:11), and his worth is incomparable.

10. Because of God's Calling of Laborers

The efforts of the past and of the present to make disciples of Muslims are justified by the fact that God has called and is still calling men and women to dedicate themselves to this specific task. They were convinced that becoming missionaries to Muslims was not by their own choice, or because of a decision of a mission board, but because of God's command to them. Somehow God laid the needs of Muslims on their hearts, and impelled them to go to some part of the Muslim world to serve, either in their own country or abroad. When anyone says that missionary time and money should not be wasted in the effort to convert unresponsive people, their reply is, "God told us to do this, we must obey God." So obedience becomes more important to them than success. They have learned to assent to the say-

[1] Rasooli and Allen, *Dr. Sa'eed of Iran* (Grand Rapids: Kregels, 1958), p. 175.

ing, "Duties are ours, results are God's." When a visitor from America asked Dr. John Elder in Iran how he had been able to spend more than forty years of his life in a land where converts were few, he replied simply, "Because God sent me here." As long as God calls servants of his to this task, who can say that the undertaking should be abandoned as useless?

But why should God send his servants to spend their lives in labors that often seem futile? Why did he send Isaiah to unrepentant Israel, a "disobedient and contrary people," who always reject God's loving appeals? (Isa. 65:2; Rom. 10:21). Why did he send Jeremiah to a career of suffering and failure? God knows what he is doing, and it is not for us to question but to obey his will. If God should send one of his servants to a barren field, where he would spend his life witnessing faithfully to Christ without the encouragement of seeing a single conversion, that would be his highest privilege, and he at last would hear his Master say, "Well done, good and faithful servant!"

11. Because of God's Testing of His Church

It seems that God in his inscrutable wisdom has allowed Jews and Muslims to remain in unbelief to test the faith and obedience of his Church. The attitude of Christians toward the multitudes who deny the deity, the finality, and the sufficiency of Jesus Christ is a clear revelation of the quality of their faith and love. Those who truly believe in the only Son of God, and who love their neighbors as themselves will take no rest till all who are now living and dying without Christ have had the opportunity to know and believe on him. The failure of the Church to tell the Good News throughout the Muslim world may indicate that when weighed in God's balances it will be found wanting (Dan. 5:27).

12. Because of the Presence of the Holy Spirit

It has been suggested that the failure of missionaries to "bear much fruit" and to produce many converts, resulting in a mass-movement of Muslims toward Christianity, is an indication that the Holy Spirit is not present in such a situation. But is this true? Is not the Spirit present wherever faithful laborers are plowing and sowing and waiting, just as he is present when others are gathering in the harvest? If there is only one Christian witness in a city filled with unbelievers, who pours out his soul in prayer for the lost, and who courageously shows Christ's love in his life and speaks Christ's message with his lips, truly the Holy Spirit is operating in power in and through that man or woman. And this gift of the Spirit is the seal of God's approval on the witness that is being given to Christ.

13. Because of God's Purpose

The conversion of any individual, be he pagan, Jew, or Muslim, is a miracle performed by the Spirit of God. For no one can call Jesus "Lord" and believe in him and become a child of God

without the work of the Holy Spirit (I Cor. 12:3).
Paul plants and Apollos waters, but it is God who
causes the seed to grow. However much Christians may have failed in their duty to evangelize
Muslims, the long delay in the conversion of Muslims is because in God's eternal plan and purpose
the time for their ingathering has not yet come.
In writing about the unbelief of Israel Paul says:
"I want you to understand this mystery, brethren:
a hardening has come upon a part of Israel, until
the full number of the Gentiles come in, and so all
Israel will be saved" (Rom. 11:25-26). May we
not think that in the same way a "hardening" has
come to the people of Islam, and in God's time
those whom he has chosen will believe, and like
the people of Israel be saved?

Then should we say that since the time for the
conversion of Muslims has not yet come, we have
no responsibility for trying to lead them to
Christ? Not so! God is now giving his Church
the opportunity to be obedient, and to help prepare the minds and hearts of the people of Islam
for his miracle of conversion which will one day
be performed. "How are they to believe in him
of whom they have never heard? And how are
they to hear without a preacher?" (Rom. 10:14).
There will be no harvest without a previous plowing and sowing and watering.

The coming of God's harvest is sure. But how
long must this preparation continue? As long as
God deems it necessary. His ways are not our
ways, nor his timetable ours. A thousand years
are with him as one day. We become impatient

if results do not soon appear, but God has eternity in which to accomplish his purpose, and he will not fail or become discouraged. He knows that in his good time the long winter will pass, the snows and ice will melt, the springtime will arrive, the seed long lying dormant in the soil will sprout, and at last the harvest will come. Today God wants us his servants to gather the stones, to plow the hard soil with deeds of love, to sow the good seed of the gospel, to water it with tears and if need be with the blood of martyrs, and in patience to wait. Those who have the high privilege of laboring in Muslim lands need never become discouraged, for though they may have little of the joy of reaping, they will have much of the joy of hoping and believing, as with the eye of faith they see from afar the glorious ingathering.

14. Because of God's Promises

We will continue to pray and work for the salvation of Muslims because we believe the promises of God. We remember that our Lord said: "This gospel of the kingdom will be preached throughout the whole world, as a testimony to all nations; and then the end will come" (Matt. 24:14). Before the end of the age and the appearing of the Son of man from heaven, the Good News will be proclaimed in all the world, including the Muslim world. Though nearly 2,000 years have passed this has not yet been done. For this "preaching" involves more than a distribution of tracts or a radio broadcast, important as these may be. It is equivalent to the terms Jesus used when he said: "Go into all the world and preach the gospel to the whole creation" (Mark 16:15). If we fail to preach the gospel throughout the Muslim world, may not we by our disobedience delay the final victory of our Lord?

This proclamation of the gospel will not be in-effectual. True was the vision which John saw on Patmos of "the great multitude which no man could number, from every nation, from all tribes and peoples and tongues, standing before the throne and before the Lamb . . . crying out with a loud voice, 'Salvation belongs to our God who sits upon the throne, and to the Lamb!' " (Rev. 8:9-10). Yes, every Muslim land and every Muslim language will be represented in that glorious company of the redeemed, clothed in the white robes of Christ's righteousness.

And when Christ returns in his divine glory with all his holy angels, then all Muslim knees will bow not toward Mecca but to him, and all Muslim lips will confess that he is Lord, some with joy, and some with shame and anguish, because of the wrath of the Lamb (Phil. 2:10-11; Rev. 6:15-17).

15. Because the First Fruits Guarantee the Harvest

In Iran we had an old Persian book entitled *Sweet First Fruits,* which told of Muslims who had been gathered by God into his Family. How many Muslims have since the time of Muhammad been given a new birth and become children of God no one but God knows. Their number may be greater than we suppose. Many in recent times in Indonesia have become members of the Christian churches. But no doubt in other lands also through the centuries there have occurred numerous miracles of conversion, the records of which are found only in heaven. Accounts of some more recent conversions are found in the books *Ten Muslims Meet Christ* and *The True Path* (see the Bibliography). All these "Sweet First Fruits" guarantee a great and glorious harvest in due season. What God has done for some he will do for many.

16. Because of the Beneficial Influences of the Gospel

It must not be supposed that, since the number of converts to Christianity in most parts of the Muslim world has till now been small, the Christian effort has been of no value. On the contrary, a great deal of service that honors Christ has been performed by Christians, both national and foreign. Missionary and national doctors and nurses in hundreds of Christian hospitals in many of the Muslim lands have treated in the name and with the blessing of Christ untold millions of Muslim patients, and have helped to train thousands of doctors and nurses who in turn have served their own people. As they have healed the sick as Christ commanded his disciples to do, they have by deed and also by word given their testimony to their Lord. Christian educators also in many hundreds of schools and colleges have in the name and spirit of Christ trained hundreds of thousands of

Muslim youth, inspiring many of them to serve their people with a truly Christian spirit, even though they may not themselves have become members of the church. In times of earthquakes and famine and pestilence and floods, Christians have assisted the afflicted peoples, and have even laid down their lives to give relief to Muslims.

Partly as a result of the presence and labors of foreign missionaries, tremendous changes have taken place throughout the Muslim world. The governments of Muslim countries, following the example of the Christians, have established hospitals and training schools for nurses and schools and colleges where formely there were none. Women, partly through the tireless efforts of graduates of Christian schools, have to some extent in some countries been emancipated from the confinement and injustices imposed on them by Islam. The health of the population in most countries has been much improved. The proportion of literates has increased. Efforts have been made by enlightened Muslims to care for people formerly much neglected—the lepers, the blind, the orphans, and the beggars. A lady who had graduated from a Christian school in Iran, but who had not herself become a church member, once said to me when I commended her for her tireless efforts to help the poor of her city, "I learned it from the missionaries!"

A by-product of the service of missionaries from the West, which was not at all their purpose in going to Muslim lands, has been the creation of large numbers of friends in those lands for the countries from which the missionaries came. A college professor in Iran once said to me, "You American missionaries with your small budgets and your limited personnel have done far more to create good relations between my country and yours, than has your government with its thousands of representatives and its expenditure of many millions of dollars."

In a lecture before the Royal Asiatic Society in London in 1927, Sir Arnold Wilson, who was then British high commissioner in Iraq, made this statement: "I should not like to speak about the Persian Gulf without bearing testimony to the wonderful work the missionaries are doing. . . . [The Arab] does not despise but greatly respects those who devote their lives to the spreading by example and teaching, the Christian religion. There is no greater influence for good in the Persian Gulf than the Christian missions; no Europeans are so universally respected as are the missionaries such as Zwemer, Van Ess, Harrison, and Mylrea."[2] He should have added, "and their noble wives."

Conclusion

What, then, should be the attitude of us Christians toward the task of making Christ known to the eight hundred million Muslims of the world? It should be one of faith and hope and love: faith in Almighty God, the "God of the Impossible," who moves mountains and is today working out

---

[2] Dorothy F. Van Ess, *Pioneers in the Arab World* (Grand Rapids: Eerdmans, 1974), p. 1.

his eternal purpose in the Muslim world; hope in the promises of God, the "God of Hope," that the day will come when every knee will bow to Christ, and every tongue confess that he is Lord; and love that never fails toward the people of Islam who have not known the love of Christ, a love that is Christlike and is poured into our hearts by the Holy Spirit, a love that will create in us a passionate longing for Muslims to know and love Christ crucified and risen from the dead, a love that will constrain us to labor for their conversion, and to say with all sincerity, "Our hearts' desire and prayer to God for them is that they be saved!"

> Now to him who by the power at work within us is able to do far more abundantly than all that we ask or think, to him be glory in the church and in Christ Jesus to all generations, for ever and ever. Amen [Eph. 3:20-21].

BIBLIOGRAPHY

"Al-Bashir," *The Bulletin of the Christian Institute of Islamic Studies,* Hyderabad, India, Vol. III, Nos. 3-4 (July-December, 1974).

Apostle to Islam, Biography of Samuel M. Zwemer, J. Christy Wilson, Sr., Baker Book House, 1952.

The Balance of Truth, C. G. Pfander, republished in Beirut, 1974, sold by Fellowship of Faith for Muslims, 205 Yonge Street, Toronto, Canada M5B 1N2.

Beliefs and Practices of Christians, Explaining Christianity to Muslims, William M. Miller, M.I.K., Lahore, 1973, sold by International Students, Inc., Colorado Springs, Colo.

Borden of Yale '09, Mrs. Howard Taylor, China Inland Mission, 1926.

The Call of the Minaret, Kenneth Cragg, Oxford University Press, 1956.

Christ in the Art of Hussein Behzad of Iran, published by the United Presbyterian Church, 475 Riverside Drive, New York, N.Y.

Dr. Sa'eed of Iran, Rasooli and Allen, Kregels, Grand Rapids, 1958.

How a Sufi Found His Lord, John A. Subhan, Lucknow Publishing House, 1952.

Introducing Islam, J. Christy Wilson, Sr., Friendship Press, New York.

Islam, Alfred Guillaume, Penguin Books, 1962.

The Koran, translated by J. Dawood, Penguin Books.

The Koran, translated by J. M. Rodwell, Everyman's Library, 1918.

The Life of Muhammad, Rev. Canon Sell, Christian Literature Society of India, 1913.

The Life and Religion of Mohammed, James L. Merrick, Boston, 1850.

Mohammed: The Man and His Faith, Tor Andrae, Harper and Row, Harper Torchbooks, 1960.

Mohammedanism, Louis Gardet, Hawthorne Books, 1961.

Mohammedanism, H. A. R. Gibb, Oxford University Press, 1968.

Muhammad the Prophet, Dr. Mahmoud Hoballah, The Islamic Center, Washington, D. C.

The People of the Mosque, L. Bevan Jones, Baptist Mission Press, Calcutta, 1965.

Religions in a Changing World, ed. Howard F. Vos, chapter on Islam by William M. Miller, Moody Press, 1959.

The Rocky Road to Mecca, Taher Ben Jelloun, Atlas World Press Review, April 1975, pp. 20-22.

Ten Muslims Meet Christ, William M. Miller, Eerdmans, 1969.

Torch for Islam, Biography of G. H. Harris, Malcolm R. Bradshaw, Overseas Missionary Fellowship, 1965.

The True Path. Seven Muslims Make Their Greatest Discovery, Mark Hanna, International Doorways Publishers, Colorado Springs, Colo., 1975.

Your Muslim Guest, Fellowship of Faith for Muslims, 205 Yonge St., Toronto, Canada M5B 1N2.

The Way of the Prophet, David Brown, The Highways Press, London, 1962.

The quotations from the Bible are from the Revised Standard Version.

The quotations from the Koran are from Rodwell's translation.